CRYSTAL WISDOM

Spiritual Properties
of
Crystals and Gemstones

DOLFYN

The ideas in this book are not to be understood as directions, recommendations, prescriptions or advice of any kind. The information in this book is based on traditional and contemporary crystal and gemstone lore. This book only intends to report that lore. Readers with medical, psychological or physiological problems should consult thier physician, psychiatrist or qualified health professional. The author and publisher do not intend that the reader rely on crystal and gemstone lore as a substitute for medical, therapeutic, psychiatric or psychological care or advice.

Earthspirit, Inc.
d/b/a Sacred Earth in California
6114 LaSalle Ave., Suite 362
Oakland, CA 94611

ISBN: 0-929268-14-8
Library of Congress Catalog Card Number: 89-83447

Cover Photo by Dane Penland

CRYSTAL WISDOM

Spiritual Properties
of
Crystals and Gemstones

DOLFYN

Illustrations by Larry Wells

Earthspirit, Inc.
d/b/a Sacred Earth in California
6114 LaSalle Ave., Suite 362
Oakland, CA 94611

WORKSHOPS WITH DOLFYN

Dolfyn teaches workshops and classes on Nature Spirituality and Shamanism in the San Francisco Bay area and nationally. For information, write: Earthspirit, Inc., 6114 La Salle Ave., Suite 362, Oakland, CA 94611

Earthspirit, Inc., distributes **DOLFYN'S BOOKS, BOOKLETS, CHARTS AND WALLET CARDS TO WHOLESALERS.** For a wholesale catalogue, send your tax #, address and $1.00 to: Earthspirit, Inc., 6114 La Salle Ave., Suite 362, Oakland, California, 94611

The public can order this book by sending price of book plus $2 shipping, handling to above address. Try your local bookstore first. Bulk rates also available.

TABLE OF CONTENTS

CHAPTER I
PRACTICING:
MASTERING THE ESSENTIALS

Crystals, especially quartz crystals, express the unity of the four elements in their very being, with nothing added to them. They are obviously of the Earth: they grow in the Earth and suggest the mineral evolution of this planet. Because they can transmit a piezo-electric charge, they are also expressions of fire. They are related to water both in their molecular structure and in their ice-like appearance. And just as air lets light pass through its clarity, so do crystals. In relating to crystals, then, we are relating to concrete embodiments of the four elements — the elements of ourselves and everything around us. So when you carry a crystal around with you, you're carrying all the elements of creation itself, in your pocket or hung around your neck. Their beauty speaks to the child within

1

each of us and invites us into the mystery or spirit realm that resonates in and through the elemental and etheric stuff of our world and ourselves.

Many people assume that interest in crystals and crystal lore has come about as a spinoff from the human potential movement or New Age thinking and practice. In short, they assume crystals are just another middle-class diversion, another fad. No assumption could be more mistaken. Primal and rural peoples all over the world have used crystals from before recorded time to heal themselves and their animals and to strengthen their spiritual abilities to enter psychic realms closed to everyday perception. Fortunately, at least some of this wisdom gathered by shamans and healers and seers has come down to us through countless generations and is being renewed among us today.

What you will find in this book, therefore, comes from an unimaginably ancient tradition, but a tradition which is very much alive today. It is a heritage which you can become part of, which you can enter as deeply as you wish. This is your invitation to add to this heritage and to make it your own by creating new expressions of basic crystal practices from your intuition, knowledge and deep wisdom. The suggestions for getting started you will find here are just that — suggestions. You should not feel bound by the suggestions in this or any other book but should be as free as your imagination allows you to be.

SIMPLE ADVANCED CRYSTAL WORK

How can crystal work be both advanced and simple at the same time? Advanced crystal work comes from the heart and the emotions. It does not take superior intellect to work with crystals at an advanced level. What it takes is so simple that, for the most part, modern people have overlooked it.

Advanced crystal work involves communicating directly with the crystal as you would with a close friend, incorporating intuition, creativity and play. It involves forming a relationship with crystals and opening ourselves to being guided by the crystal itself. It is deepening our connection with crystals and with all of life.

We all have the ability to communicate with crystals. We begin by paying attention to our imagination since crystals speak to us through non-verbal images, body sensations, heart feelings and "ideas" that pop into our minds as we hold a crystal.

Everyone who has an imagination can communicate with crystals directly. Unfortunately, it is just this sacred part of ourselves, our imaginations, that the dominant society teaches us to suppress. We learn early on not to trust the very faculty which filled us with delight and wonder when we were children and which connects us to the spirit realm now. But psychics and crystal "experts" pay attention to the promptings of their imaginations to receive and interpret detailed messages from crystals. You can, too. The crystals you work with will help you reclaim your imaginative intuition. And the crystal journeys in this

3

book will also help you learn to communicate directly with crystals and the spirit world by helping you exercise your sacred imagination.

For example, when Joan of Arc was being questioned by the authorities, they said, "Joan, don't you realize that the visions you see and the voices you hear are just your imagination?" And Joan replied, "Of course it's my imagination. God speaks to us through our imaginations."

In a similar way, when you are holding and working with your crystal, anything you think or feel or any ideas you receive are not "just" your imagination. It's your imagination with a capital I, the sacred and spirit part of you through which the spirit world speaks to us all.

The growing popularity of crystals has led to a great many books about them. Some of these books seem to suggest or even categorically state that there's an "incorrect" and a "correct" way to work with crystals. This gets quite confusing since no two authors seem to agree exactly on what is correct.

Let me assure you that there is no incorrect way to work with crystals. The only thing you can do wrong is approach crystals with the intention of doing harm in any way. As long as you do your crystal work with positive, life-affirming intentions, you are free to interact with your crystal in any way that expresses your own spontaneity and creativity.

Working with crystals is a folk art or folk science. This is not a field where one person is the authority. How we humans communicate with and work with crystals has been developed with the aid of the crystals themselves. And each of you will add to this wisdom as you work with crystals.

Furthermore, there are no valid recipes for working with crystals, the kind that give lockstep instructions and insist that you follow that recipe for the rest of your life. That is why this book emphasizes direct communication with the crystal, for each crystal is an individual. You and the crystal will mutually develop your own unique ways to work with each other to help in the healing and wholeness of life and to add to the fund of crystal wisdom.

Start off with the crystal communication exercises and crystal spirit journeys you will find in this book. And I urge you to <u>do</u> these exercises, not just read them passively. If you'll keep a crystal in your hand or nearby as you go through these chapters in a quiet, private place, you can participate fully in the new possibilities you encounter here — as you encounter them. Soon you will be creating your own style and your own methods of working with crystals.

TUNING AND COMMUNICATING

It's best to start with a clear, single-terminated quartz crystal (a crystal having only one point). Ask the store owner to let you hold it in your hand and see if you feel anything. You will feel drawn to the one that's right for you; and the one you feel drawn to is the one you should get. Remember that you may not be drawn to the most beautiful ones. If a banged-up crystal calls out to you, that's the crystal that has chosen you. The crystal will choose you, not you the crystal.

Crystal Wisdom

A crystal about three inches long and an inch in diameter, one you can easily hold in your hand or carry in your pocket, is the best size to begin with. It should be large enough so that you can gaze into it but small enough to carry wherever you go. After you've gotten such a crystal, live with it for a while. Keep it with you all the time. When you're sleeping, hold it in your hand or put it under your pillow. Meditate with it, gaze into it, look at the moon through it, look at the world through it, talk to it, say your prayers into it.

When tuning a crystal the most important thing to keep in mind is that you are attempting to form a mutually respectful relationship with that crystal. Tuning and communicating are not things you do to a crystal, they are things you do with a crystal. They include any positive activity that helps you bridge the communication gap between the animal and mineral clans. Sing to your crystal. Tell it your problems, your dreams, your thoughts. Carry it with you wherever you go and basically participate in life with it.

Carrying your crystal around is a way of tuning to it. But there are other ways of tuning you may want to try also. Any way you discover to play actively with your crystal will help you communicate and tune to it. For example, you can let the crystal rest in potted plants and see if it enjoys being there. You might sit in the sunlight with your crystal for part of each day, take it outside with you in the rain or bathe together in a stream, lake or ocean. Introducing your crystal to your favorite places, to the weather, to the seasons, will help you tune to the crystal and will open up the magical intuitive child in you — the part of your being which best communicates with a crystal.

And, of course, tuning to a crystal means listening in return. You can listen to your crystal with your body. When you first begin communicating with crystals, this is often how they make first contact with you. As you begin to tune to a crystal, you will come to realize that the individual crystal you are tuning to has its own unique talents and abilities; and a crystal will often tell you what those are through your body.

Exercise: Listening with the Body

Lie down or sit comfortably. Hold a crystal in your hand. Close your eyes. Take a few deep breaths in, and as you breathe out, let your body completely relax . . . Mentally ask your crystal what its specialty is . . . Now simply be aware of any feelings anywhere in or on your body: tingling, heat, itching or any other sensations . . . When you feel something, place the crystal on that spot and ask the crystal what this means . . . When you are through, thank the crystal for communicating with you.

It is usually easier at first to get the body sensation than it is to get the message about what it specifically means. If this was the case with your first attempt, you might figure it out after the exercise. For example, if you feel tingling in your feet, this could mean that this crystal will help you find your path. If you felt heat in your hands, this might be a healer's crystal. If you felt something in your throat, this could be a communications specialist, and so forth. Simply hold the crystal in your hand after the exercise and allow ideas to run through your mind. The first idea you get on this subject will probably be the appropriate one.

You might consider some spontaneity in tuning to your crystal: share a visualization or draw pictures for your crystal; dance for your crystal; emote with your crystal.

Tuning to a crystal is really just taking the time for you and your crystal to get to know each other fully.

Exercise: Tuning with Dreams

Place a crystal under your pillow at night. Just as you are about to fall asleep, ask the crystal to communicate with your subconscious mind, your dream self . . . Upon awakening, while you are still partly asleep, ask your crystal to help you remember and interpret any dream messages . . . Now place the crystal on your third eye (middle of the forehead) with eyes still closed. Let any words, feelings or visualizations come to you . . . Finally, give thanks to your crystal and give thanks to your dream self for communicating with you.

CLEANSING

Many people feel that a crystal should be cleansed of unwanted or negative energy as soon as you obtain it or on a regular basis thereafter.

Some of the most common cleansing and clearing practices are: burying a crystal in sea salt from one hour to one week; placing a crystal in a stream, pond, or ocean;

placing it in salt water from one day to one week; burying it in the earth from one day to one week; visualizing white light entering into and cleansing the crystal; taking in a deep breath, visualizing the cleansing and then blowing hard on the crystal, blowing away the negative energy. This list grows as people find various cleansing methods that work for them.

I feel that it is best to look at cleansing and clearing your crystal as another opportunity to interact with your crystal. For example, the water and sea salt method is the most common cleansing method. If it appeals to you, why not take the crystals into the bathtub with you when you bathe, add a pinch of salt to the water and bathe together?

On the other hand, I have found that crystals which still have earth, dirt or clay adhering to them from the ground they originally grew in are the most powerful crystals. I don't cleanse these crystals at all because the harsh chemicals that are used to remove the dirt also remove the Nature Spirits or Devas that live on the surface of the crystal. These spirits work in conjunction with that crystal to make it powerful and to keep it protected. If your crystal has no original dirt on it, you can reinfuse it with Nature Spirits by rubbing a little earth on the crystal while asking the Nature Spirits to come back and live on the crystal again, protecting it and keeping it clear of all negative energy.

Also, crystals will cleanse and protect each other, so it is a good idea to obtain a number of crystals and keep them near each other.

Finally, some people do not concern themselves at all with cleansing crystals, while others feel it is only needed if the crystal is used therapeutically on a large number of different people.

If you feel that cleansing is important to your own crystals and the work you do together with them, experiment until you find a method that suits you and your crystals. By staying in communication with each crystal, you will soon learn what each needs and feels comfortable with.

CHARGING

Charging a crystal means, simply, giving the crystal the opportunity to refresh its power to focus, enhance and direct energy. As you might imagine, there are many ways to go about this, but all of them involve a combination of intuition and action.

For example, if you wanted a crystal to be charged with the energy of cleansing, you would first of all communicate that intention to the crystal. (Some people do that ritually by speaking or chanting the intention aloud; others prefer mental communication or imaginative visualization.) Then you would place the crystal in an environment you associate with cleansing—a clean, fast-flowing stream, for instance—and leave it there for a while.

Other examples include charging a crystal with the power of emergence or rebirth by placing it in a cave, a burrow or a hollow tree stump; charging a crystal with the power of growth by leaving it for a day in a bed of healthy young seedlings; charging it for fruition by bathing it in a high tide or with the powers of rest and composure by letting it be washed in a low tide.

Practicing: Mastering the Essentials

The lunar and solar cycles also present powerful opportunities for crystal charging. A crystal left overnight in the rays of the new moon would become charged with the energy of hope, enthusiasm and new beginnings. One charged in full-moon light would be a crystal of abundance, love, giving and nurturing. The dark of the moon, on the other hand, would be a good time for charging a crystal you want to use for meditation, introspection or divination.

The cycles of the sun also present their unique occasions for specific kinds of charging. A crystal charged at the fall equinox would hold the energy of harvesting dreams; at winter solstice, the energy of rebirth and renewal; at the spring equinox, the energy of youthfulness and surging growth; at summer solstice, warmth, passion and joy.

It is, of course, much better if you participate with your crystal in the charging. So walk beneath the full moon, swim in the ocean, meditate under the dark moon, be outdoors at the equinox, wade in the stream, lie in the grass or go camping in the woods with your crystal. You will both be charged. You also need to be charged and refreshed so that you can project the love that your crystal infuses you with in order to serve the light.

In the process of charging and refreshing a crystal, you will learn to go into nature more often. You will come to learn that Earth Mother is the healing connection for both you and your crystal. This, indeed, is the crystal connection. For crystals are leading us back into nature to be healed by her and to heal her in return.

Go into nature often with your crystal. You will form

a closer bond with the crystal, with nature and with your own spirit. And you will find healing and wholeness as you connect with Earth Mother.

Again, these are only some guidelines to help you get started. Essentially, you can charge any crystal by communicating your intention to it and taking some appropriate action with it. These are the basics. The rest is up to you and your imagination.

INSPIRING AND PROGRAMMING

I regret my part in popularizing the term "programming" a crystal. The word seems to imply that a crystal is a computer or a tool with no spirit or consciousness of its own. Programming would be a good term to use if people did not misunderstand it and translate it into a use-centered, unfeeling concept. I am now trying to switch over to the word "inspiring" in talking about these matters, for it is not as charged with negative meaning as "programming." I now use these terms interchangeably.

You can inspire a crystal to hold your intention. Because crystals focus, direct and amplify energy, they will help you manifest whatever you put into them.

Basically, when you inspire a crystal, you are asking it to hold your desire, wish, thought form or prayer; and to focus and enhance your intent back to your higher self, as well as project it out into the universe. This is a participatory process; for as we inspire or program a crystal, the crystal is simultaneously programming us to raise our spiritual awareness, our clarity, our honesty and our wisdom.

Practicing: Mastering the Essentials

Of many ways to inspire crystals, these are among the most common: as you hold the crystal in your hands, mentally visualize a picture of what you want to happen. For example, if you want to program the crystal for your own good health, you visualize yourself in glowing health. If you want to inspire a crystal for solving a specific problem, visualize that problem as solved. Then picture that visualization flowing into the crystal. Someone suffering a sore back, for example, might visualize himself or herself running and jumping and then put this visualization of that healthy, active self into the crystal. As this is done, some people say words such as "I am healthy, I am healed" aloud or silently.

Another way to inspire a crystal involves holding the crystal near your heart and feeling that which you want to program into it. See those feelings going into the crystal because crystals understand pictures and feelings very well. When the words go along with the pictures, it works much better than using words alone. Further, you can chant your intention into a crystal because simple rhythm and rhyme increase the effect of the programming.

For example, suppose you want your crystal to help you make an important decision. You might make up a simple, rhythmic chant such as, "The Earth is fair, the sky is wide. Help me decide, decide, decide;" and repeat it over and over. Or you might just repeat an abstract concept over and over, e.g., "clarity of thought, clarity of thought. . . ." Close your eyes and let yourself go, rocking back and forth, clapping your hands or even dancing as you chant.

Other commonly used methods to inspire a crystal are:

drawing a picture of your intent and placing the crystal on the picture; blowing your intent into the crystal with your breath; placing the crystal on a book or a photograph that conveys your wish or intent; placing the crystal on a symbol that conveys your wish or intent, such as a Jewish star, a cross or an ankh. Many people combine one of these processes with asking the crystal to hold, amplify and focus their wishes and desires.

An excellent sequence for inspiring a crystal would combine the verbal, the visual, the tactile and the emotional.

Exercise: Inspiring a Crystal

Breathe deeply and center yourself . . . Hold a crystal in your hand and ask it to hold onto, focus and amplify your wish . . . Now verbally state what it is you want . . . Now touch the crystal to the middle of your forehead and visualize yourself having that wish come true . . . See it as if it is happening in the present moment . . . And let yourself feel good about the wish coming true . . . Send all this into the crystal and visualize your wish going out into the universe . . . Thank the crystal when you are done.

Because there are as many ways for people to program and inspire a crystal as there are people and crystals in the world, no one way is correct. It is the crystals themselves that have revealed these methods. They inspire each person with a mindset or method they can relate to easily. The method you use, therefore, is nowhere near as important as your intent. If your intentions are life-affirming and charged with positive energy, you can rely upon your creativity and your sense of play to open up the best ways for you to inspire your crystals. Ultimately you will want to develop your own methods of mutual inspiration with your crystals.

TOOLING

You can, like many ancient and primal peoples, incorporate crystals into the tools and paraphernalia you may use in healing, meditation, religious ritual and so forth. They can be sewn on garments or embedded in rings, pendants, bracelets and coronets. They may be used in rattles (small crystal chips), hung from drums and flutes, built into the stems of goblets or the hilts of knives. But among the most widely used of all crystal implements are wands and pendulums.

Traditionally, wands were slender lengths of wood tipped with a crystal of suitable size. Modern wands are often made from lengths of copper or silver tubing because these metals are excellent conductors of energy. If you decide to make a wand, use it as an extension of your body to channel energy. Treat it with respect and use it carefully as it is a very powerful tool.

By far the most common crystal tool, however, is the crystal pendulum. Crystals have been simply tied to pieces of string or suspended by a chain from a length of thin copper wire wound tightly around the crystal's base. A bell cap from a rock shop or craft store can be glued to the base and hung from a string or chain as well.

Most often people use crystal pendulums, point downward, to deal with yes-no questions. Make a simple pendulum and ask a yes-no question. Hold your pendulum by the string and allow it to become still. Think and feel the question. Focus on that question, but do not move your hand. In a short while you will see your crystal begin to move. If it goes counterclockwise, it's no; clockwise it's yes. (Some people, rather than using a formula, will work out the yes-no code with their crystal and will know what means yes and what means no.)

The crystal pendulum, with its ability to give a yes-or-no answer, is commonly used for divination, for diagnosis or for finding answers from deep within.

Pendulums work because crystals are linked with the collective subconscious of all the world. When you ask a crystal a question, you are consulting not only your own intuitive wisdom but the wisdom of all creation.

RESPECTING, THANKING, APPRECIATING

I have been dismayed to see much current crystal lore suggesting that crystals are tools to be used by us. You do not use crystals, you form relationships with crystals. And I hope you will learn to respect all life, all nature, as you learn to respect and interact with your crystal.

Crystals are conscious beings who share this beautiful planet with us. Crystals are our teachers, our helpers, our guides. They have chosen to make themselves known to large numbers of people at this time because the Earth and her human children are in great need of healing.

Of the three clans of Earth—the animal clan, the

mineral clan and the plant clan—the mineral clan is the oldest. As the oldest of all the clans, the mineral clan has witnessed human development on earth, our very evolution. And of all the minerals, the crystals have reached the greatest clarity of evolution. In that clarity, they are helping and guiding the rest of life on earth towards the light.

Each clan has something great to offer as we grow towards the light, including the human clan with its unique strengths. So let us not think in terms of using our clan brothers and sisters—the animals, plants and minerals. We are all children of Earth Mother. Let us interact with respect for each other. And let us learn how to communicate with each other. The crystals themselves will help us learn how to do this.

Here is absolutely the most important understanding you need to make part of yourself in order to communicate with, tune to and relate with crystals: everything is alive. Rocks are alive. They are living beings with their own consciousness. The waters live every bit as much as the trees do. Fire, wind, mountains, flowers and animals—all the planet's natural beings—live on and with the Earth and enliven the Earth.

The human beings who knew this in their hearts and bones as well as their heads built their entire cultures on that knowledge. Today we call these primal or tribal peoples—those who lived and continue to live close to the earth, the seasons and the stars. And these aboriginal, indigenous human inhabitants from every continent have worked with crystals for as long as there have been humans on the earth. These people include Native Americans and all the tribal peoples of the Earth.

Adopting this world view opens us not only to direct communication with crystals but also to direct communication and friendship with all of nature. As our world truly becomes alive, we become more fully alive. We wake up to the fact that this planet we live on, this Earth, is a lovely and enchanted place. All life becomes sacred to us, and Earth Mother herself becomes sacred to us. This is the mindset we want to develop for communication with crystals and for making our lives on earth more resonant with spirit: every natural thing on earth is alive and has consciousness.

In the primal world view, we are related to all life. The animals, plants and minerals of the earth are our relatives. We can communicate with all of them. But because we are also the youngest and newest life on this planet, we must communicate with the other living beings on earth to make our lives more whole and balanced through their guidance, help and teaching.

Out of our deep respect and appreciation for the crystals and for all life, it is important that we always thank the crystals whenever we work with them—not because the crystals need our thanks but because the very process of thanking opens up something in us that's healthy and necessary for our spirits. Our lives become better in all ways when we have a feeling of gratitude in our hearts towards all life.

For all these reasons, I urge you to state your thanks simply and from the heart each time you work with your crystal.

CHAPTER II

EXPANDING: REACHING BEYOND THE BASICS

MEDITATING AND GUIDED CRYSTAL SPIRIT JOURNEYS

If you already practice some kind of meditation, it will be enhanced by involving your crystal in it. Many people like to place a crystal over their third eye, which is in the middle of the forehead, and then begin meditating in their usual way. But almost any kind of introspective activity—calming, centering, trancing—will be deepened by the presence of a crystal, especially one you have inspired to help you in that area.

If you haven't tried meditation yet or have a hard time at it, your crystal can be especially helpful. You might, for example, take a hand-held size crystal and, either sitting or lying down, just gaze into it. Because it's so beautiful and hypnotic, because it has so many complex and interesting worlds within it, it can draw you into an altered state. In that altered state, you may then choose to put the crystal down and go into a deep meditation. Or you may keep the crystal in front of you for continued gazing.

Those who meditate by gazing at a candle flame might try suspending a crystal on a string so that it hangs in front of the flame, in the line of sight.

Moving meditations such as Tai Chi, yoga and Sufi dancing are also augmented when the meditator wears a crystal or keeps one nearby.

Again, these few suggestions are offered mainly as aids to your imagination. But no matter how you make use of crystals in meditation, you will find your crystals a powerful ally in your journeys into your deepest self. After all, as has been stressed before, making connections are what crystals are all about.

Guided meditations or spirit journeys are one of the easiest ways to meditate. They are also one of the main ways in which we communicate with crystals, and they communicate with us. Our spirits need to journey in other dimensions, which is why we dream and daydream—to note two common examples. The intentional interdimensional journeys presented here give our spirits the healthy nourishment they need.

The inner vision quests or guided meditation crystal journeys interspersed throughout this book give you the opportunity to journey to the spirit world. There you will meet your spirit helpers, the crystal spirits in their many guises—and your own higher self. There you will learn to tap your own deep wisdom so you can bring it back and make it part of your everyday life.

Important as these guided meditation journeys are, it's also important that you don't try too hard to make these journeys happen. You'll go where you need to when you are ready to. There's no need to force it. Some people "see" the journey; some "feel" it; some sense it in a way they can't describe. Most people wave in and out of the inner journey and their minds wander in between. That's fine. Since you can't force your spirit to do anything, you might as well just take it as it comes. If you fall asleep in the middle of a journey, that's fine, too. Your subconscious mind knows well where to go from there. In fact, going on a spirit journey just before you fall asleep at night is a good idea, for at this time you are very receptive and open to the spirit world and to communication with crystals.

Undertaking a crystal spirit journey requires little special preparation. But because your attention will be elsewhere, you should not attempt such a journey while you are driving or in any situation where you need to be alert. Go on these journeys where it's quiet and where you can relax, lie down and close your eyes.

The guided meditation journey is a suggestion. Feel free to launch off on your own spirit journey at any time during it and trust your higher wisdom and your crystal to take you where you need to go.

Some people simply read the journey to themselves and then close their eyes and go. On the other hand, you might want a friend to read you these crystal journeys or you might read them into a tape recorder and play them back to yourself. Read them in a slow, calm voice. Three dots (. . .) mean a long pause.

The first crystal spirit meditation journey presented here begins with a thorough relaxation exercise to help you enter the journey. You may choose to use this extended relaxation exercise before entering the other journeys in the book, or you may find that you don't need it. Experiment until you discover how you best establish the relaxed state needed for these journeys.

The same holds true for the directions used to return to ordinary reality from a spirit journey. You may choose to use the very gradual method I've provided at the end of this first journey. Or you may find you're comfortable with the more abbreviated versions which end the other journeys. Of course, if you are making a spirit journey as a transition to sleep, ignore the return directions entirely.

Finally, if you go on guided spirit journeys often, your spirit will eventually begin to travel where it needs to spontaneously—without a guide.

Spirit Journey: Meeting Crystal Spirits

Lie down and hold a crystal in your hand or place it somewhere on your body. Close your eyes and get comfortable. Start breathing deeply. With each out breath, let yourself completely relax. Let your shoulders drop. You deserve these few moments of deep relaxation . . . Visualize, think or feel that you are walking down a path in the woods, a forest path. And as you walk you can hear the birds singing, you can feel the breeze and see the dappled

Expanding: Reaching Beyond the Basics

sunlight through the trees. You can smell the fresh, clean smell of the forest. And as you walk in this quiet, serene place you grow calmer and calmer, more and more relaxed . . .

Now you see in the distance a large cave. It looks interesting and inviting. You come up closer and enter the cave, and you walk deeper and deeper, down into the cave, into the heart of Earth Mother. You notice that you feel more and more relaxed as you go. You realize that the deeper you go, the more crystalline the cave becomes; and the more crystalline it becomes, the better you feel. Now you are actually inside a huge crystal. You look around at the beauty with wonder. Now go explore this crystal world where you may meet wise and friendly people, animals and other beings, or where you will simply feel and understand the energy . . .

Now as you become ready to return to the mundane world, bid farewell to the spirit beings that you met . . . Start walking upwards in the cave. You feel happy to have gone on a crystal journey. You are walking up, closer and closer to the cave entrance. You leave the cave and are now walking on the forest path back to where you came from. And as you come back, you become more aware of your body. You realize that your toes and fingers need to move. You wiggle them and you feel very good. You stretch your body and feel refreshed and relaxed. When you are ready, open your eyes and sit up.

HEALING

One of the primary ways that crystals have helped humankind has been and is the effort to heal. Because crystals are themselves whole, they want us and our world to be whole.

Crystals have been used in healing for so long, by so many different people and in so many different traditions (some of them very sophisticated), that a huge and complex body of knowledge about these things has emerged—so much that it can be overwhelming. You'll find in talking to experienced crystal healers that you quickly get into very complex discussions about such things as chakras, polarities, cycles and layouts. And you can quickly feel lost. You shouldn't be cowed when that happens. No matter what you may hear or read about complex metaphysical and physical healings systems, it's basically something direct and simple: in traditional healing, the crystal is placed on or near the place that needs to be healed. In other words, people place a crystal on or near the afflicted area. And as they do that, they inspire the crystal to heal that specific problem.

Common crystal lore has it that the base of the crystal held over an afflicted area will draw out negative energy; the point held over that area will send in positive healing energy. Again, as this is done, the crystal can be programmed by saying things such as "Heal and be well."

Because most people can't go around all day holding a crystal on the part that hurts, many crystal users will inspire a crystal for a specific or general healing and then simply wear it in a pouch or on a chain or carry it in a pocket.

Expanding: Reaching Beyond the Basics

Still others have created various devices to hold crystals on or near problem areas: bracelets to hold the crystal next to the arms or legs, crystal-studded belts to be worn near the abdomen and even bandaids placed over tiny crystals on the exact part of the body that the crystal is needed. In addition to applying a crystal to the affected area or wearing the crystal on the body, some people pass a crystal over and around the afflicted area, while holding it in their hand. Waving a crystal over the body in sweeping arcs is also used to cleanse the body's aura, restoring imbalances in the body by correcting the imbalances on the auric plane.

Yet another approach to self-healing with crystals has to do with alignment. Crystals are placed around a person at the four cardinal directions, their tips pointing inwards. As the person sits quietly or lies in sleep, the crystals invite the body's energies into alignment with the energies and forces of the planet and the universe.

A very direct and simple method of healing with crystals is one of the most common methods used. A crystal is held in the hand while going to sleep. The crystal is asked to heal during sleep, by working with the subconscious mind. Using this method, people often report that, while asleep, their hand has moved the crystal to exactly the body area that needs healing.

In addition to using crystals for physical health, you may also want to try some common practices which are often used to enhance mental and emotional well-being. One simple method of achieving emotional balancing involves lying on the back while holding a crystal in each hand and resting another small crystal on the forehead.

Crystal Wisdom

Some people just rest in this position for a comfortable period of time, while others prefer to visualize or feel the interplay of the crystal's energies with their own mental and emotional energies. Gradually, the person begins to feel all these forces coming into equilibrium with each other.

Rather than trying to "fix" various emotional moods with a crystal, you might prefer a more wholistic approach. Because crystals help people get in touch with all the various hidden parts of themselves, they help people to balance by helping them see their negative or shadow aspects. Being in contact with crystals, it is believed, allows the unowned, hidden, unconscious parts of the self to come into the light—to be integrated, connected and brought to a healing wholeness.

Because crystals themselves come out of the matrix of darkness in the Earth, all crystals (but especially the smoky and milky quartzes) are especially suited for giving people the courage, the wisdom and the patience to get to know the deep, rich, unconscious part of themselves. It is that part of the self which tends toward destructive expression when it remains unacknowledged, unrecognized and excluded from conscious integration into the whole being. Its energy becomes twisted and distorted into such things as hostility and depression.

And while there are no quick fixes, no recipes for eighteen different ways to conquer depression with crystals, there is another kind of relationship to depression and loneliness that can be entered into simply by being with crystals. Working with crystals may lead a person to discover that depression and fears and worries aren't necessarily things that have to be conquered or overcome, as this dominance-loving culture seems to suggest. A person may instead find that these things are part of life for some reason, perhaps as an invitation to some new kind of growth or some new kind of re-energizing. Crystals are very good at putting us in touch with such possibilities.

In an alienated society like this one, if you need a friend, you've got one in a crystal. And when you have one friend, often there's a healing that allows you to go on and make other kinds of friends. In a lonely society crystals are there to talk to, to love and be loved by. Not only does your loneliness lessen, you may experience a healing that lets you make more intimate contact with people again.

If you tend to be nervous and a worrier, you have, in a crystal, something that can protect and calm you. As you feel safer and happier in the world, you may be able to reconnect with the world in a more trusting and friendly way.

To summarize, people commonly use one or more of these ways to heal with crystals: The crystal is placed on or near the area of the body that needs to be healed; the base of the crystal is placed on the afflicted area to draw out the negative energy; the point of a crystal is placed over the affected area to send in healing energy; the crystal is held while falling asleep and asking the subconscious mind to direct the healing energy; crystals are aligned in creative and intuitive ways on or near the person to be healed; crystals are waved around the body in large arcs; a crystal pendulum is twirled over the chakras or simply twirled in creative, intuitive ways over the body; various crystals and other gemstones are arranged on the body in systematic or intuitive ways. The list goes on, limited only by each healer's intuition and inner wisdom.

To open up your own intuition and inner healer, healing meditations and crystal spirit journeys are most helpful. Here is an inner journey to help you tap your own intuitive healing wisdom and energy. You might want to go on this journey just before you send healing energy through a crystal.

Spirit Journey: Medicine Crystal

Lie down, holding a crystal in your hand. Close your eyes. Breathe deeply and relax . . . Imagine that you are walking down a forest path at dusk. As you walk, it grows darker and darker. As it does so, you become more and more relaxed . . . The moon is full. It lights your way as you walk in beauty under the night sky. Ahead, in the distance, you see a bonfire burning in a clearing. As you walk closer, you see a large circle of crystals surrounding the fire. Inside the circle are people. As you approach, you see that these are people of an older time, yet they look very familiar to you . . . They are of all different ages. This is a group of people that you feel akin to. You would like to join them . . . And as you walk towards them, you realize that you are now wearing the sort of clothing they wear . . . As you approach, one of the people notices you and smilingly beckons you to join them. With a sense of joy and belonging you step forward, into the crystal circle, and join the people . . . Everyone is happy to see you. They crowd around you and welcome you . . . Now a wise old person hands you a crystal and tells you to heal with it.

Expanding: Reaching Beyond the Basics

*You look around and realize that at the edge of the circle
a mother is cradling and rocking a sick child in her arms
. . . Hold the crystal over the child, sending healing energy
through the crystal. As you do this, the crystal begins to
glow. Now you begin healing in an intuitive manner with
the crystal . . . The child stirs, becomes alert, smiles and is
healed . . . The mother and all the people rejoice . . .*

*Now it is time to return. Bid farewell to the people
and, if you intend to return, let them know this. Give the
healing crystal back to the old wise person to be held for
you until the next time you return . . . Give thanks to the
people, the crystal, the circle and the forest . . . Now walk
back along the path you came . . . As you walk, the dark
turns back to light in the forest . . . You feel refreshed and
centered as you return to the earth plane . . . When you are
ready, open your eyes.*

We must also remember that our own healing does not
and cannot take place in isolation. Because we are part of
the Earth, we cannot be healed and whole while our Earth
Mother is sick and hurting. Nature is in crisis now, being
hounded and destroyed all over this lovely planet. We are
children of the Earth; each of us is a tiny cell of her body.
Healing Earth Mother, protecting her plants, animals and
wild places, is a necessary part of healing ourselves and
other humans.

Exercise: Healing Earth Mother

*Bring a crystal to a natural body of water (a stream,
pond or ocean) . . . Program, inspire and pray to the crystal
to help the waters of the Earth run clear and pure again.*

Visualize white purifying light going into the crystal . . . Dip the crystal in the water and send healing thoughts of love into the water . . . You can either take the crystal home again or drop it into the water as an ever-present healing gift to the Water Spirits and to Earth Mother.

Healing the earth with the aid of crystals can be done in any natural place. For example, you might place a crystal at the base of a tree, sending healing energy and protection to the wild places, to all our green brothers and sisters and to all the animals who dwell in the wild places.

As we heal and protect nature, we find our own lives becoming whole. Let us also protect our sacred Earth Mother in mundane and practical ways. True healing begins with healing Her.

PROTECTING

To live in an environment created by an urban, industrial culture is to live in an environment filled with stressful assaults on the human organism: pollution, noise, microwaves and wave after wave of negative emotional energy generated by those stresses. And the people who live in the midst of these stresses, disconnected as they are from the elements, are especially vulnerable to these stresses. But because crystals express elemental wholeness and connectedness, they are especially useful in countering the negative effects of artificial environments. In fact, after healing, protection seems to rank as the next most frequent use of crystals today.

Expanding: Reaching Beyond the Basics

When you talk to crystal people, almost invariably they'll tell you they have a little quartz or amethyst cluster that they wear on a chain as a piece of jewelry, keep in their pocket or in a little bag around their neck, or just leave on their desks. Using these decorative and protective amulets or talismans is really very easy and requires no complicated thinking or planning. Quite simply, you can inspire a single crystal or a cluster to provide protection and then keep it with you or leave it in your home or your workplace. Many people program several crystals for this purpose, spreading them around their various work and living areas, wearing one or more and even keeping one in the car.

Crystals inspired for protection don't prevent negative energy from being produced, but they deflect that energy away from you. In other words, they help you perceive the negativity that may come your way and help you let it flow on by without it affecting you. And while amethysts and clusters are considered especially effective at deflecting and dispersing negativity, any crystal will do if you're well attuned to it. Some people even tell of their crystals cracking as they "took a hit" for their wearers, as they shielded the wearer or user from extremely negative forces.

It is important, however, if you are using crystals more or less exclusively for this purpose, to reconnect with those crystals from time to time and to let them refresh and charge themselves in the kinds of elemental conditions you're using them to stay connected with: earth, air, fire, water.

It is likewise important that we learn to cooperate with

protection crystals to accomplish their work. Because such crystals are about re-establishing the balance of energies in the world around us, we have to become more aware of our own role in creating those energies. It is unrealistic to expect crystals to shield us from the negative effects of human intentions and actions if our own intentions and actions are helping to create the imbalance. For example, if we were to work with a crystal to protect ourselves from environmental pollution while we continue to drive where we could walk or to patronize businesses that use "throwaway" plastic containers, we would be asking that crystal to protect us from ourselves!

Similarly, if we ask a crystal to guard us from the negative emotional energy directed at us from another person without having tried to resolve our problems or to achieve reconciliation with that person, we may be asking that crystal to do the impossible. After all, crystals are always seeking balance and connection. Those of us who work with them should try to do no less.

PROJECTING ENERGY AND PRAYING

If someone you know and care about is undergoing some kind of difficulty or suffering and you want to send them your prayers and good wishes, crystals can enhance this process. This is called projecting energy through crystals.

Crystals channel, focus, project and increase any energy that you send out. So when you pray, if you direct your prayer into a crystal, the crystal will enhance that prayer. You can visualize the prayer going out of the crystal and into the universe, among all the forces of the cosmos.

When you want to send a prayer of healing for the earth, for people you know or for an area of conflict in the world, it is good to do that through your crystal. But you can project any kind of energy through a crystal, and it will be magnified. For example, if you need money, you could place a crystal on a ten-dollar bill and project energy by praying, through the crystal, for what you need. Make sure, however, the energy you project through a crystal is only positive energy because whatever you send out will come back to you—magnified many times. This is a universal law. If you send harmful, negative energy through a crystal, you will be harmed far more by the energy returning to you. On the other hand, if you send healing and loving and positive energy to other beings and the Earth, then you will be healed.

One way of projecting energy through a crystal is to hold it out at arm's length, point it to the sky and send your prayer and your feelings into the crystal. Visualize them going up through the crystal and see these prayers and feelings coming out as light that enters the universe, that flows like water from a fountain over the entire universe. You send your prayer through your body, into the crystal and out to the universe. To project energy as a group, have a number of people sit in a circle with a crystal in the middle. Everyone then puts their hands on or near the crystal and sends their intent, their will, into the crystal by visualizing white light entering the crystal. The group can also chant the intention into the crystal rhythmically. Crystals greatly enjoy singing and chanting.

FOCUSING: CRYSTAL SHRINES AND ALTARS

People often set aside one area of a room as a focal point of crystal energy, where they place many crystals. These focusing areas are sometimes referred to as crystal altars. The very act of setting up your crystal altar can be a process of connecting with all your crystals and can be done in a manner that induces a calm and meditative state.

You can also incorporate other beautiful and inspiring things from nature such as seashells, a houseplant or a piece of driftwood. Thus your crystal altars also can serve as a reminder of the beauty and sacredness of the Earth. Some people also include on their altars a statue of a deity or a picture of a human or animal friend.

These altars may be quite simple (a few objects arranged unobtrusively on a windowsill, for example); or they may be quite elaborate and involve an entire room. Many people set aside a table low enough to kneel or sit in front of as an altar.

As you sit before your altar, you can meditate, pray or send healing energy. Or you may simply gaze at, touch and hold the crystals and other natural things on your altar. In this way you permit yourself to daydream, communicate and intuit with the crystals and with your highest self.

Furthermore, you can use this altar to center your crystals and yourself with symbolic representations of the four elements—earth, fire, water and air. For example, you might place upon your altar a bowl of water, a candle, a feather and a houseplant. Thus the crystals, and you too, can be continually balanced and recharged by the healing wholeness of the elements of nature.

You may also want to create permanent or temporary crystal altars outdoors in a place where you go to meditate or just to relax. These outdoor altars (or shrines, as they're often called) are usually one or more crystals placed in a streambed, on a rock ledge, or in any quiet place. Such natural settings usually require no additional decoration, although some people leave prayer ribbons or other offerings at these shrines when they visit them.

GAZING: SEEING THE STARLIGHT VISION

Because crystals are in such a state of perfect balance themselves, they induce balance in all who keep them near. Most people from our culture have not developed their intuitive, spiritual side as compared to their mundane side. Crystals, therefore, encourage an awakening of our visionary and psychic selves. To see with the Starlight Vision is to see the whole, the gestalt, in a lyrical, heart-centered way. Understanding the universe in this manner is conducive to clairvoyance, divination, telepathy, forecasting, scrying and so forth.

Crystal gazing can help enhance psychic knowing. Basically, gazing simply means looking into the crystal in some concentrated way. To do this, you will need a crystal at least three inches long and an inch in diameter, and it would help to have one larger than that. It should be large enough to see into but not so large that you can't comfortably pick it up and turn it around as you are lying down.

Crystal Wisdom

Within your crystal you will discover various fractures and formations, referred to as faerie frost. It looks like fuzz, wisps of hair or clouds that are typically most dense near the base of the crystal and gradually taper off into the clear portion of the crystal's shaft. These cracks, chips, lines and bubbles create endless worlds within the crystal; and the more you gaze into them, the more complex and entrancing these worlds become.

As you hold your crystal in your hands for scrying, slowly turn it before your gaze. The crystal's beauty will draw you inside it where you may see shapes, landscapes, worlds, people, animals, faeries and other beings. From some of these beings you may get a strong feeling of familiarity, a realization that you know them well. Some may speak to you, and some may communicate with you through your feelings. You can ask questions as you look. Some will be answered in pictures you see; some answers may come at the level of feelings. It's a way of entering other realms, perhaps realms of concurrent time and space, of the past or of the future.

To develop your psychic abilities further, guided crystal spirit journeys can be very helpful. You might want to take this journey just before gazing into a crystal or engaging in any form of divination or psychic activity.

Spirit Journey: Awakening the Starlight Vision

Lie down, close your eyes and relax . . . Imagine that you are walking under the night sky . . . As you walk, the stars glow brightly above, and you become more and more transfixed by their beauty and mystery . . . You are now ready to lie down and gaze at the stars . . . As you lie there, you begin to notice one specific star that seems to be glowing brightly just for you. The star becomes brighter and brighter as its beam shines down upon you and surrounds you in its glowing light . . . You are filled with happiness, and so you rise up and dance in the starlight. You dance with a freedom you've never felt before. You dance to express your love of life and your oneness with the universe . . . And as you dance, you notice the quality of light has changed. You look closely at the light beaming down to you from the star—there are now small bodies, tiny planets, suns and stars moving in the light. And these tiny celestial bodies dance with you in the beam of starlight and move around you . . . And as you watch them, they grow a little larger until they are big enough to climb upon. You hop upon a small planet and ride up the beam of light. This is an exciting, wondrous ride to the stars. Enjoy it. Look around you. Feel the exhilaration . . . As you approach the star, you see a beautiful Star Goddess reaching out to you. As you come closer to her, she touches your forehead with a crystal and says, "See now, my child. See with the Starlight Vision." As she touches you, you feel the tiny stars, moons, planets and suns entering you and filling you with their power, with their knowing, with their glow . . . Allow these tiny worlds to enter you, allow the universe in and open your self to the Starlight Vision . . .

When you are ready to return to the mundane world, bid farewell to the Star Goddess. If you want to meet her again, let her know this. Give thanks to her, to the Crystal Spirits and to the stars and planets . . . When you are ready, open your eyes and stretch, feeling refreshed and alert.

CELEBRATING

Celebrating and giving thanks are very important things for humans to do because these activities remind us, in fundamental ways, of who we are and what we value. These times of celebration and thanks are traditionally called rituals or ceremonies. Whether we go in for the traditional rituals our culture or our religion offers us or whether we create our own, crystals can greatly enhance the process.

Crystals are especially helpful in rituals and ceremonies because they want to bring things into harmony, which is the purpose of most rituals: to celebrate or re-establish a harmonious relationship with people, divinity, our higher selves, nature and so forth.

Among many primal peoples, quartz crystals are valued for a variety of rituals, especially those that have to do with the well-being of the group or individuals. They are frequently used by healing shamans.

Let your crystal participate in any traditional ceremony or ritual that is meaningful to you. Some examples: In a wedding ceremony, the couple might charge crystals with love and exchange them. Or you might hang a crystal on your Christmas tree and charge it with peace on Earth. Or again, after you light your Chanukah candles, you might meditate on the candle flames, looking at them through a crystal. And then you might inspire the crystal with the energy of freedom and hope which this ritual celebrates.

Crystals can provide a focus for self-created rituals of joy and life affirmation, for rituals that connect us with

38

life and connect us with our deep selves, for rituals that make us whole. Some examples of self-created rituals include sitting within a circle of crystals and praying for abundance, balance and wholeness; then picking up each crystal, touching various body parts and asking for something you need. For example, you might pick up a crystal, place the point to your forehead and say, "Grant me wisdom to understand and know the mysteries." Or you might place another crystal at your heart and ask for love, tender emotions or whatever you need to make you whole.

Another self-created ritual could involve Earth healing. You might charge a crystal with healing and then bury it in the earth as you visualize healing energy going out to all of nature.

Again, your imagination is the only limit here. You might link your crystal rituals with the phases of the moon or the seasons of the year and renew, at these times, your thankfulness, joy, and commitment to the highest good. Let the rhythms of nature herself suggest the appropriate rituals—spring for rebirth, fall for thanks, the new moon for the hope of new beginnings and so on.

Crystal Wisdom

CHAPTER III

DEEPENING: EXTENDING
YOUR REACH

ENCOUNTERING CRYSTAL TEACHING
SPIRITS

When a highly evolved soul, a teacher, guide, shaman
or wise person moves on to the spirit world, they often
choose to be reincarnated into a crystal—and not only
human spirits but highly evolved animal and plant spirits
as well. For example, the leader of a wolf pack, the
medicine wolf of that pack, may have reincarnated into a
crystal. Or the spirit of a big grandfather oak tree that
passed into the spirit world might also be present in the
crystal. And that is one main reason why crystals are
becoming so popular now. They have chosen to live with
and teach so many of us at this time because we are in need

of real spiritual teachers and wise guidance.

Some crystals have more than one teacher within them. A crystal teaching spirit can become a close personal friend who has specifically chosen you to guide and work with.

Crystal teaching spirits may make themselves known in sudden, dramatic ways, or they may choose to reveal themselves very subtly and gradually. Some of these teachers present themselves most sedately; others love to clown and laugh. Some appear frequently, others only rarely. The manner of their appearance and their teaching style matter less than what they have to teach us.

The following exercise is one way to begin getting to know the teaching spirit or spirits inside a crystal.

Exercise: Seeing the Crystal Teaching Spirit

Lie down or sit comfortably. Hold up your crystal so that you can gaze into it. Ask the crystal spirits to communicate with you . . . Now gaze into the crystal as you turn the crystal all different ways. You may see, in the fractures and planes inside the crystal, a picture of a human, animal or plant. This is one of the teaching, healing spirits who have reincarnated into the crystal. Ask this great spirit to be your teacher and to communicate with you and guide you . . . Now put the crystal on your heart and see if there is a message for you at this time . . . Be sure to thank the crystal and the teacher spirit or spirits when you are through.

Another way to contact the teaching spirit or spirits inside your crystal is to dance them in.

Deepening: Extending Your Reach

Exercise: Dancing in Crystal Teaching Spirits

Hold a crystal in your hand while standing. Breathe deeply and begin to move spontaneously. You might also speak, chant, pray or sing—focusing upon calling in the crystal teaching spirits to move through you. For example, you might say something like, "Crystal spirit teacher, I invite you to dance with me."

As you move, an image, idea or feeling of an animal, plant or person may come to you. Begin moving and making appropriate sounds for that being. For example, if the idea of a bear comes to you, move and vocalize like a bear. If the crystal teacher is a Bear Spirit, you will find that it will help animate and energize your movements and voice. Really let go and express Bear Spirit with energy. At the point you feel the energy has peaked, stop moving, stand, sit or lie down and listen with your heart for a message.

The teaching spirit inside the crystal enjoys experiencing embodied movement like this from time to time. Therefore, when you dance in the teaching spirit, not only do you get to know it well, you also provide a joyous experience for both of you.

PLAYING IN A SACRED MANNER

It is difficult to teach playful spontaneity in a book. In my workshops I can demonstrate with humor, with light-heartedness and sometimes even with ecstasy that a human and a crystal can communicate fully, intimately and easily. Just seeing one person do this is most freeing and invites my students to do the same. Within a short time all the students are directly interacting with their crystals in a wonderful mixture of respect and playfulness. In print, all I can do is assure you that if you interact with your crystal in a spontaneous manner, you will not only reap the benefit of the healing friendship that crystals have to offer, you will also begin to open to creativity, joy and ecstasy in all areas of your life.

Just as our imaginations are sacred, so is our creative play. Connecting with a crystal in laughter and joy is a great gift you can give the crystal and yourself. Let your inhibitions go. Be playful, be silly, be joyful—do whatever comes to mind as long as it's life affirming. For example, I often gather a group of crystals together and play-act with them. I pick up each crystal, spontaneously speak its part of the dialogue out loud and extemporaneously act out its part in the play. This might sound ridiculous, and it can be . . . but it also has, at moments, opened me up to channeling directly a verbal message from each crystal. And when it's not revealing, it's just downright fun.

Crystals are also most attractive to beings more comfortable with playing than the average adult human usually is. Many people comment that children and pets seem to enjoy being around crystals, and that's to be expected. But you may also discover that elves, faeries and other such playful creatures will make their presence known when you free the child within yourself as you play with your crystals. When you notice fleeting movements at the edges of your vision or that a spirit of merriment suddenly surrounds you and your crystals, chances are some of these beings have come to join in the fun!

Crystals are beings of great joy; and if you will open to their guidance, they will teach you to play with them creatively in a sacred manner. They will teach you that laughter and play can be just as sacred as prayer and meditation.

BRIDGING PAST AND FUTURE LIVES

According to some teachings, we each live many different lives on this earth. Other belief systems hold that we experience different lives simultaneously on differing energy planes or in various parts of the universe. Some people believe in reincarnation or parallel existence as actual realities; others understand such beliefs as poetic expressions of the unrealized potentials of a single, earthly lifetime.

Although our individual beliefs about such matters may vary, crystals are constant in their ability to help us explore and experience those beliefs. As elementally whole beings, crystals are not bound by divisions and limitations of time, space, dimension or perception. They are structured to make connections among various mani-festations of energy and to transform one kind of energy into another. Therefore, they are ideal space-time bridges between the past and the future, the potential and the actual.

Crystals can help us get in touch with our past lives

and with our future lives as well. They can help us remember incarnations on earth as well as on other planets, galaxies and star systems. They can help us understand the persons we were and are and might become. This information is good to have because it helps us integrate our current life with our soul's journey.

Spirit Journey: Crystal Time Bridge

Lie down, close your eyes and relax . . . Imagine that you are walking down a path in the forest . . . It is peaceful and serene. As you walk deeper and deeper into the forest, you grow more and more relaxed, calm and centered. As you walk, you see in the distance a bright and shimmering crystal bridge that spans a wide river . . . As you draw closer to the bridge, a feeling of timelessness engulfs you . . . And as you step upon the bridge, you realize that you have come to a place in reality where there is no such thing as time.

You are aware, as you walk across the bridge, that you are walking to other lifetimes, to previous or future lifetimes. As you walk the crystal time bridge, you begin to feel very good, very happy to be on this journey. And as you walk upon the crystal bridge, a mist rises up from the water and surrounds you . . . As you come to the other side of the bridge, you see that it leads to high cliffs that are enshrouded by the mist . . . As you step off the bridge onto the cliff, you peer down to the valley below. The mists begin to clear as the scene and the person or people you see in the valley below become clearer and clearer . . . Now you may go down the cliff for a close view and interaction, or you may stay on the cliff and observe . . .

When it is time to return, give thanks to any people you met and give thanks to the crystal bridge . . . If you intend to return, tell the people of your intent . . .

Now walk back the way you came, feeling refreshed and happy to have made this spirit journey . . . When you are ready, open your eyes.

GROWING

Don't hang around with crystals if you are afraid of growth and change because transformation toward the light is what crystals are all about. There may be times when that transformation process is scary or even painful. But your crystal can help you open to the wisdom of seeing that this is sometimes necessary for further growth to occur.

Your work with crystals, for example, might bring you face to face with habits or mindsets you need to cut loose in order to become a more whole person. It might bring into your consciousness old hurts which have been buried for a long time, so that they might be healed. It might show you that happiness and success are not defined in the ways the mainstream culture says they are. It might sharpen your sensitivity to the suffering of other beings and of the Earth herself. Yet genuine growth, genuine transformation inevitably demands such periodic disillusionments and awakenings. Learn to accept them, for these kinds of experiences ultimately bring true wisdom.

Crystals are also about balance, and you can aid this

process by staying aware that your crystal is constantly guiding and inspiring you toward balance. Needless to say, a crystal is a good friend to have along in all therapeutic and counseling situations.

Probably the most important point to emphasize about growing, transforming and balancing is the necessity of staying open to the mystery of crystals, and my experience as a teacher and an author leads me to offer these words of caution. Too many people who teach and write about crystals describe their own beliefs and practices as if they were universal laws. One crystal teacher, for example, might insist that you must wash your crystals in salt water once every ten days for twenty-four hours, or bad energy will get you. Another teacher might insist that unless you breathe white light on your crystal, nothing good or powerful can take place.

Such prescriptive approaches to crystals seem to inhibit growth and promote fear. If you encounter such insistence on recipe-like rituals that have no particular meaning to you, ignore them and put your trust in your own deep wisdom and creativity, knowing that you are sustained by an abundant and joyful universe.

I offer this guideline for those in doubt: if it's not joyful, creative, generous and loving, it's probably not a universal law but simply a reflection of a given teacher's doubts and fears.

Finally, instead of continually trying to work your will upon the crystal, let yourself be open to what the crystal has to teach you. I suggest that crystals be perceived as friends, teachers and guides on the many paths toward the light.

Deepening: Extending Your Reach

Spirit Journey: The Crystal Seed

*Lie down, close your eyes, and get comfortable . . .
You are going back to the crystal cave for a new journey.
Again, as you walk deeper and deeper down, down into the
cave, you feel serene and relaxed . . .*

*Now, as you approach the main section of the cave,
you notice a little side cave. You peer into it, and it is dark
and mysterious inside. You are intrigued by this small
cave, so you enter . . . As you go down deeper and deeper,
it becomes more and more dark until the only light that you
can see is a small blue glow in the middle of the cave. You
go over to it and you see that it is a tiny seed crystal, a little
seed that is also a crystal. You pick up the blue, glowing
seed crystal; you cup it in both your hands. The seed
crystal lights the way as you walk toward the cave exit
. . . You peer outside and see a beautiful garden. You step
into this garden and immediately feel the power and the
energy of this place. The birds sing in the trees; a small
brook runs gently through the garden; the leaves of the
trees dance and glitter in the wind and the sun . . . You see
a bare spot of dark, fertile earth, and you realize that this
is a good place to plant your seed crystal. As you plant it
in a sacred manner, you pray for that which you hope to
grow . . . You pray for something you need now, something
you need to plant in your life . . .*

*Now it is time to return to the mundane world. Give
thanks to the spirits of the garden; give thanks to the tiny
seed crystal . . . When you are ready, open your eyes and
stretch. You feel awake, alert and refreshed.*

GOING ON

After you have had the chance to try out some of these ideas, you may well find yourself becoming more and more involved with the spiritual qualities of crystals. You may find it helpful, as some people have, to keep a journal of your experiences or to talk over your discoveries with friends. Either way, you will become more and more conscious and intentional in your use of crystals. And you will very probably want to learn more about them.

If you're scientifically inclined, you may want to look into the geology and minerology of crystals, visiting museums of natural science and perhaps even prospecting for crystals on your own. (Your state geologist's office can guide you here.) But if you want to explore the spiritual and healing aspects of crystals even further, you should ask at metaphysical bookstores and other alternative culture businesses in your area to find out about workshops or seminars to attend. Anyone who sells crystals, crystal jewelry or crystal books should be able to help you.

By far, though, the most appropriate guides for further crystal exploring are your own imagination and your own curiosity—working, of course, with your crystals themselves. When you've begun to find benefits from one kind of crystal practice, stay open to suggestions about how to expand that practice, especially those ideas that come to you while you are working with your crystal.

At the end of this book, you'll find the author's address. If you want to share what you've learned in using this book, please write.

TAPPING OUR INNER TEACHER

The so-called authorities of this world tell us that we are making progress. Yet we don't have to look far to see that this progress is all too often an excuse for destroying our environment and our brothers and sisters. What we see behind the nuclear weapons, the vanishing animals and forests, the acid rain, the polluted air and water is greed—pure and simple.

If our reliance on outer authority is the cause of so many of our problems, how can we rely on outer authorities to find the life-giving solutions and renewed perceptions we so badly need? Like you, I have longed to find the guru, teacher, guide or medicine person who would tell me exactly what I needed to do, who would direct me on the highest and best way. I, too, have read many books and have met many teachers who claim to have the answer.

And, like you, I have never found The Answer from The Expert satisfactory. Indeed, all too often I have found that those who pretend to know all the answers are most concerned with fattening their reputations or their bank accounts, or both. So I have become very, very suspicious of outer authority, whether it be political or spiritual.

Instead, I have learned from the crystals and the crystal spirits to look within to the inner spirit, the inner power, the inner wisdom. Here, within, is the source of healing for ourselves, for all of life and for the Earth.

This is the real crystal wisdom: each of us can tap deep inner wisdom, can journey to the spirit world and return with a true vision—a vision of hope and peace and life-affirmation. And, furthermore, each of us can act on that

51

truth with courage. That is the message the crystals bring humankind, and the time to fulfill that message is now. Earth Mother needs your crystal wisdom to help her, to heal her and to save her.

I believe each and every one of you who are reading this has great wisdom to bestow upon the subject of crystals and upon all spiritual matters. Let it unfold! That is a path of spirit and of joy. Let your inner power unfold.

One of the greatest guides we have with us now is each crystal itself, and all of nature—for always remember that crystals are only one part of the greater whole, a never-ending source of wisdom, comfort and healing: our sacred Earth Mother.

May we all come into our own crystal wisdom, to heal our blessed Earth Mother as we are healed by her.

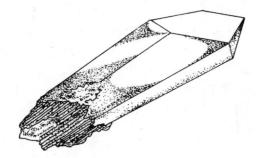

CHAPTER IV

SPIRITUAL VALUES
OF CRYSTALS

Knowledge about the specific spiritual attributes of crystals comes from the crystals themselves, filtered through the hearts and minds of those of us who work with them—and that includes you, the reader; for as more people work with crystals, additional knowledge will unfold.

Every crystal has the ability to function interchangeably with any other crystal type. So you don't necessarily need a Merlin Crystal to focus energy with, for example, or a Quartz Cluster to purify and cleanse the environment. Any crystal will do any of these things well. You may read that a Tabular Crystal, for instance, facilitates communication.   Yet, as you work with one, you find that your particular Tabular Crystal fosters dream recall, too. If this talent of Tabular Crystals is not sanctioned by the literature, ignore the books and go with your intuition.

You can't pigeonhole a crystal, and crystal stereotyping is just as silly as human stereotyping. Each crystal has its own identity. If you get to know the crystal you are working with, you will find that it can and will make its unique abilities known to you. Follow your heart with peace and joy and belief in your own inner crystal wisdom, and don't let the so-called "experts" intimidate you from doing so.

A type of crystal known to some people by one name may reveal itself to other people by an entirely different name because crystals communicate to us within each person's worldview and mindset. If a person is technologically or intellectually oriented, they might receive a crystal's name and specialty in a scientific nomenclature and definition. If a person is more mystically inclined, the crystal will speak to them in devotional terms and categories. And if the person is a gentle dreamer, the exact same type of crystal may speak to them in poetry.

Besides its clan name or type name each individual crystal also has its own personal name. Ask your crystal its name, and it will answer you in a language that you resonate with.

ABUNDANCE CRYSTALS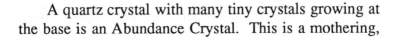

A quartz crystal with many tiny crystals growing at the base is an Abundance Crystal. This is a mothering, protective crystal, bestowing upon all who befriend her a nurturing, loving energy. An Abundance Crystal wishes all good things for life. Abundance, fullness, sufficiency and creativity are hers in plenty, and she offers these attributes freely to those who keep her near.

Abundance Crystals also foster prosperity, well-being, success, good fortune, blessings and growth. This auspicious crystal works in conjunction with Earth Mother, whose energy it facilitates. Just as our Earth Mother nourishes us with her bountiful love, so does an Abundance Crystal encourage our dreams and wishes to thrive.

An excellent way to work with an Abundance Crystal is to go to a natural place, hold the crystal to your heart and pray for abundance of any kind. Then bury the crystal in the earth as a symbolic gift for Earth Mother. The mothering crystal united once more with the all-embracing Earth from which she was born will work in conjunction with the Earth to fulfill our prayers.

These crystals also encourage us to be generous and to give freely. This is an abundant universe, and there is enough for all — if we but share.

Abundance Crystals Speak:

With ancient wisdom and mothering care,
I teach your spirit to flourish and share.

Open your arms and you shall receive
That which you visualize, think and believe.

And learn as your blossoming dreams unfold,
That a generous heart is worth more than gold.

55

AMETHYST

Violet to dark purple, Amethyst is customarily associated with increased nobility, spiritual awareness, meditative and psychic abilities and inner peace. It is valued for its ability to transform negative energy into positive energy, to bring an understanding of death and rebirth, to amplify healing, to promote altered states of consciousness and to relieve stress.

Amethyst is seen as one of the most important and powerful stones. It is the most spiritual of the stones and serves as the medicine woman, or high priestess of the mineral clan. Lady Amethyst is a strong but gentle teacher of all things spiritual, mystical, and psychic. She leads us slowly but surely into the spirit realm, where all things become possible. If you wish to experience her abilities directly, lie down on your back, place a small Amethyst on your forehead and close your eyes. She will help you enter altered states of consciousness and will guide you towards oceanic, cosmic awareness.

As medicine woman of the oldest clan on earth, she is very healing of the body, mind and soul. Lady Amethyst also is vitally interested in healing the planet. It is a good thing to pray to this lady for peace on Earth. She will send your prayers to the Creator. Pray also for the healing and saving of all the wild places and animals, for this lady loves and protects these also.

Amethyst wants humans, the youngest species on earth, to grow, evolve and transform the Earth into the paradise it can be, reflecting in all ways the Creator's wish for life.

Spiritual Values of Crystals

Amethyst Speaks:

I come to you in gentle love,
Uniting Earth with Heaven above;
Be peaceful children and never afraid,
For in love and light we all were made.

Youngest species, human child,
Learn to be gentle, loving and mild.
I teach you the ALL: birth, death and rebirth.
Together we can create Heaven on Earth.

ARTEMIS CRYSTALS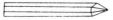

These are long, thin crystals with sharp, undamaged points (also known as candle crystals). These crystals can get us in touch with the Artemis archetype, whether you think of her as a goddess or as a metaphor for independence, freedom and love of nature. As the protectress of women, children, wild places and wild creatures, Artemis can be invoked with this crystal and her energies can be manifested in yourself.

Artemis Crystals are also very supportive of those who are struggling for independence of all kinds: economic, spiritual, creative or mental. A most freedom-loving crystal, Lady Artemis is the champion of those who are trapped or imprisoned in any way. She expresses the affirming spirit in all life that longs to be free, and she lends strength and courage in the struggle for freedom. An Artemis Crystal also encourages the inner beauty that may be trapped or imprisoned within our souls to express itself and surface into the light.

Crystal Wisdom

This crystal combines strength, action and directness with sensitivity and kindness. And like their goddess namesake, Artemis Crystals are the dynamic archers of the quartz clan. Prayers, visualizations and thoughtforms sent through this crystal fly with the speed of an arrow straight to the mark. Lady Artemis is a crystal of great focus, swift and sure. Her aim never wavers as she directs the energy to the source.

My Artemis Crystal gave me this invocation. You may wish to use it while holding your Artemis Crystal, or you may want to create your own spontaneous prayer to this freedom-loving lady:

Artemis Crystal Prayer:

Lady of the wild things—wood and hill and dale—
Steward of all freedoms, defender of the frail,
Tender of the forests, empowering the tame,
Protectress of all nature, I ask this in your name:
(state your prayer)

CHANNELING CRYSTALS

All crystals are excellent for channeling. However, some people find that a crystal wrapped in copper wire or placed in a copper dish will especially facilitate the process. Others have found that a crystal with a seven-sided front facet and an opposite facet that is an equalateral triangle is a powerful Channeling Crystal. Still others find that any crystal with a good, undamaged point facilitates channeling. I have found that any crystal—no matter the size, shape or the condition of the point—can be useful in channeling the higher forces if it is programmed and inspired for that purpose. In fact, my most powerful Channeling Crystal is tiny, chipped and visually undistinguished.

Channnneling has come to have many different meanings. Essentially, everyone is a channel. Channeling Crystals help us tap our own abilities to channel life-affirming energies and entities. There is nothing strange or mysterious about channeling. It is really just communicating. We can all communicate with the higher forces of goodness and light and with our higher selves. Channeling Crystals help us to do this. When some people define channeling, they mean going into a trance state and letting an outside spirit entity speak through them. This is certainly a dramatic way to channel, but not the only way and not necessarily the best way for everyone. I channel various light beings, but I remain fully awake and conscious. I simply place my Channeling Crystal over my heart and "hear" them with my feelings or with words in my mind. From time to time I see them also. But I can stop, walk away and move with no drama at all back and forth between the channeled state and everyday awareness.

There are other ways to channel, also. Have you ever met someone who is very loving even though they did not come from a loving home? They are channeling love energy. They are an open channel for the love energy of the universe to pass through them. Did you ever know someone with a great sense of humor, even though they came from a family of sober, serious, humorless folks?

Where did this humor come from? They are an open channel to the laughter of the universe. The Channeling Crystals allow us to open our own neurological channels to all kinds of joyful, wise, loving energies.

While holding a Channeling Crystal, ask that you become an open channel to your highest good and see what comes through. It may be an angelic spirit guide, or it may be a good joke. Both are much needed and will serve the light well. The lesson Channeling Crystals bring us is that you can learn to channel what is highest and best for you. The trance channeler is no better, no higher, than the channeler of laughter and fun. Both have their way to serve the light. Let your particular method of channeling unfold in its unique way.

CITRINE

People have long believed golden yellow Citrine to be an energizer, furthering prosperity, generosity and creative power. An expression of sunlight—warming and life-giving—it stimulates earthly pleasure, protection, strength and confidence. Citrine is considered healing to the digestion and the emotions, as well as strengthening to the body.

Citrine's golden color imparts the warmth and love of the sun, bathing all in its life-giving glow. And just as the sun is a protective father giving life to the Earth, so Citrine shares those fatherly qualities in abundance. He is protective, strong and generous. He bathes us in the light and helps us learn to always turn to truth, goodness and spirit.

Spiritual Values of Crystals

Citrine bestows the gifts of material abundance upon us, just as a father supports his children. Citrine is one of the most powerful and giving of all the stones.

When holding a Citrine, visualize yourself bathed in a golden glow of protection . . . Now visualize this glow growing until it surrounds your house . . . then your neighborhood . . . then your entire planet . . . Visualize protection and abundance for all life on earth.

Citrine teaches us that there is nothing wrong with earthly pleasure as long as it harms no life. Bathe in the sunlight; dance under the stars; walk barefoot in the grass; glory in the miracle of an incarnate body. Citrine helps us realize that it is good to enjoy life and at the same time quest for spiritual growth. Citrine opens up our awareness that this earthly plane and our bodies are gifts from the Creator. He encourages us to unite Earth and spirit and see them as one.

Citrine Speaks:

Look to the truth, look to the light;
There is no sin in earthly delight.

I help you to balance, with golden glow,
Heaven above with Earth below.

For all life is sacred, there is no doubt;
Sacred within and sacred without.

You also are sacred; your body and soul
United in love and once again whole.

So create and enjoy and affirm as you live,
And give back to life, abundantly give.

CRYSTAL BALLS

Crystal Balls reflect the wholeness and integrity of the circle, which from time immemorial has been the greatest archetypal symbol of perfection known to humankind. When a crystal is cut into a sphere, it resonates with the power of that shape. The primal peoples and those who follow a path of Nature Spirituality always worship and celebrate life within a sacred circle or medicine wheel. The circle symbolizes Earth Mother and her abundance; it reminds us that life is an endless wheel of birth, death and rebirth. And this is why Crystal Balls are much prized by those who would see the past and the future; for the circle, empowered three-dimensionally in a sphere, connects the universe and reminds us that there really is no beginning and no end, no past and no future, in the realm of spirit. We are linked to all life, with all the energy that ever was and ever will be.

Deep within a Crystal Ball is a place that is "between the worlds," a gate to other times, other realities. As you gaze at the ball, you are drawn within to worlds untold and possibilities unknown. For this reason, I suggest a ball with many inclusions, fractures, and faerie frost. These Crystal Balls are good to use in conjunction with any divinatory or prophetic activity, such as I-Ching, Tarot, palm reading, and so forth.

I find that the best way to work with a Crystal Ball is to incorporate it into your daily meditation. If you do not meditate daily, you might start now, using the ball as a focus. Sit comfortably, breathe deeply and simply gaze into the ball. If the ball is small, you might want to lie on your back and hold it up to eye level or do the same thing while seated. This has the advantage of letting you turn the ball this way and that as you gaze into it. As you look into the ball, the beauty and complexity of the world inside will draw you in, putting you into a relaxed, meditative state.

Next, clear your mind of all thoughts and questions. If the Crystal Ball wants you to see the future, it will help you to do so on its own terms. You need not push for this to happen. In fact, trying to make it happen will interfere with the process. Just be receptive to any thoughts or ideas that come to you at this time; be open to any images you see in the ball. Later, after meditation, is the time to sort through these images to see if there is a message for you. If you become analytical during your gazing session, you will lose the relaxed state and the meditation will be interrupted.

If you want to ask your Crystal Ball a specific question, you may find working in conjunction with the Fire Spirits a powerful way to do so. You will need a Crystal Ball that is small enough to turn 'round and 'round at eye level as you sit comfortably before a fire in a darkened room or outdoors at night. If you really want to enhance the prophetic powers of the ball, do this during a full moon. First write down your question on a piece of paper, then throw the paper into a fire, while asking the Fire Spirits to help you. Pick up the ball and gaze into the fire through it. (Again, I find that a ball with many fractures, planes, inclusions, and faerie frost most useful for this.)

Finally, you may enhance the effectiveness of your sessions with the Crystal Ball by working with it inside a surrounding circle of other crystals.

CRYSTAL CLUSTERS

Crystal Clusters foster protection, cooperation, participation, harmony, union, agreement and sharing.

Just as the crystals in a cluster live together in a close-knit family, so they teach us to live in friendship and intimacy with others. They encourage us to realize that we are all related.

Clusters help us satisfy our need to belong by guiding us toward our own tribe or clan—the intimate group with whom we share our daily lives. Secure in the nurturing love this group gives us, we are then able to reach out with love and healing to the rest of creation.

Crystal Clusters, living in perfect concord, tend to have the ability to break up negative energy in the environment. Many people therefore place a cluster in a home or situation that needs to become more positive and cooperative.

Clusters help keep the emotional atmosphere sweet and can also purify our minds and hearts. You can place a small cluster on your forehead, while lying on your back, to help rid your mind of negative ideas or place it over your heart to cleanse negative feelings. And for those who fear specific situations, such as flying, a small Crystal Cluster inspired and programmed for protection can offer a sense of calm and serenity.

Crystal Clusters Speak:

Animal, human, plant or stone,
None are meant to live alone.

64

From the safe sure nest of a loving clan,
You can reach out to every woman and man.

Loving, sharing, living as one;
I teach you that it can be done!

DEVIC CRYSTALS

A crystal with a great deal of faerie frost (the fractures and inclusions inside the crystal) is a Devic Crystal.

A Devic Crystal opens us to the beauty and wonder of nature and also facilitates our communication with the nature spirits—the Devas and elfin folk who dwell on the earth concurrently with humans. These Earth Spirits are very shy and elusive because they have lost their trust for man, who is destroying nature. So to re-establish communication with them, we must first do something concrete to help nature. When we show the fey folk that we are sincere, we can then expect success in communicating with them.

Once you have firmly established that you are a caretaker of nature, you might take a Devic Crystal and a gift for the Earth Spirits to a natural place. A piece of fruit is a good gift and so is a small crystal. Find a hollow in a tree, a hole in the ground or a crevice in a stone. Natural openings and hollows are faerie doors. Put the gift in front of the entrance way, without blocking it. Then sit quietly in front of the opening and speak into the Devic Crystal, telling the nature folk you come in friendship. Ask them to hear what is in your heart. Tell them of your love of nature and all that you have done to aid her, then state that you seek entrance into the Land of Faerie.

Now just sit quietly with eyes open, but in a meditative or contemplative state. If a spontaneous poem or any words come to you, say them, and then revert to the quiet meditation. If you play a musical instrument, you might bring it and play for the Earth Spirits or sing to them, for they love music and poetry. After a while you may see little flashes of light and movement out of the corners of your eyes. These are the Earth Spirits showing themselves to you. They vibrate at a higher rate than humans and move much more quickly, but this is usually how we first see the fey folk. If you do see them in this manner, be very aware of any thoughts, feelings or pictures that come into your mind, for there may be a message to you from them.

It usually takes time and sincere effort to win the trust of the Earth Spirits. Man has broken that trust again and again in his needless destruction of their natural dwelling places, and the nature folk are rightfully cautious. Yet there was a time when our species communicated with theirs. Now both worlds must meet again, for there is much we need to learn from the Land of Faerie. So it is a good thing if we humans can again live in friendship with the little people. As humans gain more respect for nature and revere her, as people work with crystals to bring us into greater alignment with nature, more and more people will gain entrance to this enchanted world.

Some of you reading this book may come from elfin stock; and as soon as you begin to initiate contact, you will know just how to proceed. It will come naturally to you, for this contact, elf-kin, is your birthright. For the rest of us, it is an honor, a joy and one of the greatest delights of living on Mother Earth.

So go into nature often with a Devic Crystal. Meditate in front of the holes and hollows that are faerie doors or inside the natural stone circles that are faerie rings. For when humans and Earth Spirits come together again in love and in trust, then together we will heal our sacred Earth Mother.

Devic Crystals Speak:

Celebrate life, laugh and sing;
Dance with me in a faerie ring!
Sing for the elfin, the little folk all:
If your heart be pure they will heed the call.

If your soul be gentle and peaceful within,
You will be accepted as faerie kin.
For you the woods will glitter and shine,
And worlds of magic will always be thine.

For you every valley and mountain and moor,
Will lead to another faerie door.
You'll walk with the fey folk hand in hand,
And the Earth will become an enchanted land.

DOLPHIN CRYSTALS

Near the base of a larger crystal there may be a smaller crystal seeming to ride along with it. This is a Dolphin Crystal. The smaller crystal symbolizes the dolphin young swimming with its mother. It is therefore a graphic representation of the protective, loving energy dolphins project toward the weak, the small and the gentle. For example, there is a place where you can pay a fee to swim with dolphins. The dolphins here show great interest in pregnant humans and can detect a fetus with their sonar. They are also very loving and protective of the handicapped children who are brought to swim with them for therapeutic reasons. It has been found that one session of swimming with dolphins can transform a person's life. Dolphins also like most women and gentle men. They do not care for aggressive people, can detect immediately who these people are and will not as readily play with them.

Dolphin Crystals can attune us to the dolphins. Dolphins and crystals have much in common. Both have a great affinity for the other and are very protective of life. Crystals and dolphins rank among the highest forms of consciousness on this planet and in the universe. The love offered by both the dolphins and their mineral counterparts, the Dolphin Crystals, is oceanic and overwhelming.

I would like to share a ritual that I perform from time to time and would like to encourage others to try: I free a Dolphin Crystal by dropping it into a natural body of water while praying that humans will let free all the captive dolphins, for these sacred beings must not be jailed in manmade tanks.

We do not need to confine dolphins physically to communicate with them. We can contact them through a Dolphin Crystal. Ask the dolphins, through your Dolphin Crystal, for wisdom, gentleness, playfulness, laughter and loyalty. Then listen for a reply from the dolphins through the crystal, for dolphins are anxious to communicate with humans for the same reason crystals are: to share their wisdom with us so that we, like them, will take up the sacred duty of protecting and nurturing all living things.

DOUBLE TERMINATED CRYSTALS

A Double Terminated Crystal is one which is faceted on both ends. In the more common single terminated crystal, the energy flows in through the base and out through the point. However, in the Double Terminated Crystal, the energy flows both ways at once. Therefore, they are considered helpful in easing the transition between alternate realities and the mundane world. Double Terminated Crystals also facilitate communication between the conscious and subconscious mind and between the heart and the mind. They promote psychic work, dream recall and the balance of body, mind and spirit.

Since Double Terminated Crystals can simultaneously project and receive energy from both ends, they help unite the mundane with the spiritual, helping us enter meditative and altered states and then facilitating our re-entrance to the everyday world again. They allow us easier access to the spirit world, the dream world, the world of our own inner feelings and creativity.

They are helpful in any form of prophetic or divinatory endeavor, as well as in astral projection. They not only open up the inner eye, they help our intuitive selves translate to our logical verbal selves—thus bridging the gap between the left and right hemispheres of the brain and allowing us to retrieve our psychic, intuitive knowledge

69

and to apply it in our everyday lives.

Double Terminated Crystals help us to walk in many worlds with balance and with ease.

Double Terminated Crystals Speak:

*Out of the spiraling, soft velvet night
I bring intuitive knowledge to light.*

*Act and then dream, awaken then sleep;
I glide in the shoals as I swim in the deep.*

*Spirit to matter, woman to man,
Cosmos to atom—I am the span.*

EIGHT-FACETED CRYSTALS

A crystal with eight facets is valued for its ability to empower and energize. It is associated with success, prosperity, and accomplishment. This stone also teaches us to balance the desire for material things with the need for spiritual attainment. An Eight-Faceted Crystal radiates great energy and power; yet as it empowers us, it guides us at the same time toward the moderate and the good. This is a most helpful crystal to have around when pursuing a business venture or planning a career, for it is success-oriented. An Eight-Faceted Crystal shows us how to put our energy to practical and pragmatic use while not losing sight of our spiritual values.

Spiritual Values of Crystals

EMPATHIC CRYSTALS

We who find ourselves seeking a crystal often assume that we will be attracted to the prettiest one, one without chips or flaws. But then we pick up a marred, strangely shaped, unclear little crystal and this is the one that speaks to us. Crystals that have been chipped and damaged are Empathic Crystals. They have developed understanding and kindness to a great degree. These crystals are the ones we can tell our own hurts to, and they will understand. They also permit us to grow in compassion for the suffering of others.

All crystals promote balance; but Empathic Crystals not only open the hearts of those who have closed them, they also protect the open-hearted from too much pain. If you are overwhelmed by someone else's pain or are too often immobilized by the pain of this world, hold an Empathic Crystal, take three deep breaths and breathe the pain into the crystal. Then bury the crystal in the Earth, asking Earth Mother to transform the pain to positive energy. Remember, Earth Mother can make flowers out of manure, and so she can also make something beautiful out of your pain. She does not mind this particular kind of negative energy because it was born of empathy and kindness to another. She loves you for feeling sensitive and caring and will help you to transform the hurt. Thus freed of immobilizing pain, you are then able to return actively to life once again.

EXTRA-TERRESTRIAL CRYSTALS

Extra-Terrestrial Crystals have a single termination at one end and multiple terminations at the other end. Extra-Terrestrials are a form of Channeling Crystals. They are especially useful in channeling the positive beings of the celestial planes—including gods, goddesses, angels and space travelers. Keeping in mind that channeling simply means communicating (often over long distances and lengthy spans of time) you will realize that the channeling crystals are simply a specific and highly focused type of communication crystal.

E.T. Crystals facilitate communication with the space beings who have visited this planet many times and are known to the inhabitants of earth as the pantheon of gods and goddesses.

Some channelers feel that it is important to bathe oneself in white light and invoke protection while channeling, so as to insure that only positive entities and energies are allowed entry. In my own way of doing this, I state out loud that I invite all sources of good and light to come forth and leave it at that. You can also readily develop your own method of clarifying and protecting during a channeling situation. Once I state my intention to communicate with positive beings, I simply speak into my Extra-Terrestrial Crystal and tell the star beings of the feelings in my heart or ask a question. I have been rewarded with visitations from the Star Goddess—a very wise and loving female entity who has been a great teacher and guide to me.

The angelic realm is also easily accessible with an E.T. Crystal. Each of us has a guardian angel—and you might want to communicate directly with yours through your E.T. Crystal.

(ARTIFICIALLY) FACETED CRYSTALS

Quartz crystals that have been cut into rings, crystal balls and pendants have the same attributes and energies as naturally terminated crystals, with one exception. Without a natural termination, they do not focus and direct energy as well. They emanate a more diffuse energy. Artifically Faceted Crystals can be helpers towards the light as much as any other crystal. But they are more likely to radiate their energy outward in all directions and not to point a laser-like, focused power, as naturally terminated crystals do. Thus, worn as jewelry, they work quite well because the wearer absorbs their vibrations. They can hold a program or be charged and inspired for a particular purpose. They can be helpful in meditating and divination (crystal balls are often used for this), and they can facilitate communication and connectedness as all quartz crystals do.

HERA CRYSTALS

Hera Crystals are also known as Self-Healed Crystals. These crystals have been broken off at one end and then have grown one or more terminations over the broken area. Hera is the Goddess of immortality, renewal, birth and rebirth. Her namesake crystal is customarily associated with all of these regenerative qualities. Lady Hera, in her crystalline form, is therefore a shaman, or wounded healer, who teaches us to tap our own self-healing powers.

Lady Hera reminds us that we are constantly in an endless cycle of life, death and rebirth at a cellular, a personal and a cosmic level. Therefore, she grants us the courage to die to the old, to make place for the new—on all of these levels. Just as the leaves fall in the winter to fertilize the ground with their decay and thereby nurture the new growth of spring, so Lady Hera helps us shed that which it is time to let go of in order to allow renewal within us.

HERKIMER DIAMONDS

These tiny quartz crystals are found only in Herkimer County, New York. They are usually double terminated and sometimes have three or more terminations.

Herkimers are considered good for promoting smooth energy flow, enhancing creativity and helping us get in touch with our own uniqueness. They foster originality of thought and are stimulating to the imagination.

Herkimers are the nonconformists of the crystal clan. They have the courage and the energy to stand alone, to express their own specialness. They impart that same energy to all who befriend them. They also have all the qualities of Double Terminated Crystals and are therefore a helpful companion in every kind of psychic work.

Herkimers are also thought of as very powerful quartz. For this reason they are considered general energizers, enlivening all who keep them near.

INNER CHILD CRYSTALS

A crystal which has another, smaller crystal partially embedded in it is called an Inner Child Crystal. The inner child, or child within, is a very important concept in psychology, especially for those of us who come from dysfunctional families—families in which we had to repress our feelings or act as emotional caretakers of our parents rather than receiving emotional nurturing ourselves.

For those of us who had difficult childhoods, there's still a child within who is sad and frightened and who needs a good parent. An Inner Child Crystal can help us go back to our childhood and heal the child within.

Spirit Journey: Healing the Child Within

Hold an Inner Child Crystal in your hand, close your eyes, breathe deeply and relax . . . Think of a time in your childhood when you really needed comfort and nurturing but didn't get it, a time when you were frightened or hurt . . . Most of us can see and feel these times very vividly if we concentrate on a specific one, because that scene is still lodged very deeply within . . . Now imagine you as you are now, as an adult, stepping into that scene and joining yourself as a child . . . Tell the inner child that he or she is not alone anymore, that you are there now, that you'll protect, nurture, comfort . . . If it's all right with the child, give comfort now with hugs and soothing words . . . Finally, invite the inner child to step out of the past and live with you in the present where you will be sensitive and kind to the child within. If the inner child is ready to do this, visualize both of you returning hand in hand, and then open your eyes when you are ready . . . If the inner child is not ready to leave that sad scene yet , tell him or her that you will return often to give help and love until the inner child is ready to live in the present. Give the inner child a protective crystal ring to wear that can be used to summon you whenever you are needed. It is also a ring of great power that will empower the inner child to be strong . . . Then open your eyes when you are ready to return.

LEFT-HANDED CRYSTALS

A crystal with an extra facet on the left side of the largest facet of the crystal is a Left-Handed Crystal. These crystals are considered to be receptive and to help us receive energy when we hold them in our left hands, on the receptive side of our bodies. These crystals activate the right hemisphere of the brain and therefore increase creativity, imagination, psychic ability and meditation. Left-Handed Crystals enable us to become more intuitive, promote emotional clarity and spiritual insight and offer us the patience and tranquility to attain our highest good.

Left-Handed Crystals are absorbent and are therefore considered able to draw out unwanted or negative energy. Finally, this crystal is a source of acceptance and tolerance, teaching all who befriend it to develop these qualities abundantly.

LIFEPATH CRYSTALS

These are long, thin crystals with one or more totally smooth sides. Run your finger up and down one. If you find no imperfections or obstructions, this is a crystal that will help you find your path in life. These crystals are also called Beauty Way Crystals.

To walk a path of beauty, a path of joy, will be the way that serves life best because it encourages your own joy and happiness at the same time.

A lovely ritual to perform each morning (and I do this one upon rising) is to touch a Lifepath Crystal to your feet and say something like this: "May I always walk a path of goodness and of light. May I serve my highest good, as I serve all life."

A Lifepath Crystal also helps us flow with the current of life. And as it does so, it encourages us to open up to our own inner flow and find a gentle, peaceful way to move forward—on the earthly, the spiritual and the emotional planes. On all three levels, a Lifepath Crystal points out the way of joy.

Lifepath Crystals Speak:

Follow a path filled with love and peace,
Walk in the sunlight with hope and with ease.
Walk in the moonlight with unending grace,
And beauty will find you in every new place.

MERLIN CRYSTALS

Merlins are also known as sending crystals, generating crystals, generators and energy guides. They are single-terminated crystals with six facets that come to a sharp and undamaged point. They have much in common with Artemis Crystals but are not as slender. Furthermore, the energy of an Artemis Crystal is extremely refined and focused compared to that of a Merlin, which projects a great blast of concentrated energy.

Merlins are the wizards of the quartz clan, sending forth powerful energy into the universe and then directing that energy so that it manifests on the earth plane for the good of all life. Merlin is a crystal of great wisdom also and teaches those who work with him to use magical powers only in ways that are life-affirming.

Most commonly, people hold a Merlin and point it to the body area to be energized or pray through it while pointing it in an appropriate direction: heavenward to the angels, earthward to the Nature Spirits and so forth.

Merlins are also used in conjunction with other stones to focus and augment their energy. This is especially useful with any crystal or stone that has no termination. For example, if you have an Abundance Crystal with a damaged point, you might place a Merlin on top of it to help direct its energy.

You may try working with your Merlin in this way: Stand with legs apart, feet firmly on the ground. Take three deep breaths and focus your own energy. Hold a Merlin above your head, arms straight. Visualize a white healing beam of light flowing out the point to a specific situation on Earth that needs positive transformation.

Merlins awaken our own powers of convergence. They are especially concerned with teaching humans to gather together in love and trust. They direct and guide energy to its highest good, and they teach us to do likewise. For just as they encourage the concentration of positive forces to energize, so do they guide us to enhance inner convergence.

Merlins Speak:

I gather together to lovingly guide
Energy far and energy wide
To one tiny point; the whole will unite
To generate goodness, to focus the light.

METEOR CRYSTALS

Meteor Crystals have a number of tiny craters indented on one side of the crystal, with a tail trailing from them. These shooting stars often fall in the same direction on any one side of the crystal.

This crystal fosters transcendence, cosmic consciousness, mystical vision, universal love and a sense of the vastness of the universe and of the soul.

Meteor Crystals have recorded the fact that we are all from the stars, that we are all star-born. From a strictly scientific view, everything and everyone on Earth is matter from a star that exploded, traveled long and far through the universe and stopped off awhile to become Earth and her citizens before moving on. We are all traveling star stuff. Meteor Crystals have recorded this so as to impart our true heritage to us. We are star children on a long adventurous journey. Our souls were forged in the heat and passion of a distant star, and this life is just a very small part of our wondrous voyage through the universe. Furthermore, Meteor Crystals remind us that every being on Earth was once one star. We are all of the same star parent. In fact we were the star parent. So all of our molecules and atoms and souls have intermingled through vast space and time. We are all truly one here! We must therefore love and protect all life on Earth as if it were ourselves, for it is!

Meteor Crystals Speak:

You were born in light, you were forged in the fire
Of passion and power and love's desire.

You have traveled long; you have far to go.
Therefore journey in peace and in love's fair glow.

For no matter who or what you are:
You are a miracle, you are a star.

MILKY QUARTZ CRYSTALS

Milky Quartz appears whitish and opaque, especially compared with clear quartz. Currently, clear quartz is more valued, and so milky quartz is much less expensive.

Milkies get us in touch with the hidden, invisible, elusive within us and without. Our subconscious minds are all creative geniuses, rich and fantastically complex.

Milkies help us tap deep wisdom from within, often the wisdom that has been denied and buried both in our culture and in our individual selves.

Milkies are good for unlocking secrets and mysteries of all kinds and are a very powerful ally for all spiritual and psychic undertakings. They're also useful in conjunction with psychological therapy to help us more clearly see into the mystery of our own subconscious dreams, desires and motivations.

Milky Quartz is highly underrated and deserves more attention. I believe everyone values the clear quartz more at this time because our culture is afraid of mystery. There is an American Indian prayer that says, "Thank you, Great Spirit, for the mystery." Milkies awaken in us an appreciation for the mystery. And in the midst of thankfulness, the veil lifts slightly, ever so briefly, to give us a non-analytical, intuitive glimpse in which we see clearly for a moment before we come back to our everyday life, itself a beautiful mystery.

MUSE CRYSTALS

A cluster of nine similarly-sized crystals, the Muses represent the nine goddesses who preside over the arts. The crystalline representatives of these goddesses promote creative expression as well as appreciation for beauty, grace and harmony in music, poetry and the arts. Muse Crystals bestow flights of inspiration and aesthetic awareness. They also open our eyes to the beauty around us, especially helping us to recognize inner beauty and truth, as well as allowing our own inner radiance to shine forth.

Muse crystals awaken us to the poetic and the lyrical in our hearts and then help us to express them in our everyday lives. These crystals are very helpful to artists, musicians, writers and craftspeople in fostering inspiration, creativity, originality and the discipline to manifest their concepts in artistic form.

Such people often keep their Muse Crystals nearby when they practice and perform, or place these sensitive crystals with their paints or in their instrument cases. We writers find that it helps to leave a Muse Crystal atop a manuscript, when we've set it aside for a while, to inspire us when we return to work on it.

MYTHIC CRYSTALS

Double-terminated, milky quartz crystals are Mythic Crystals in that they hide within their opaque beauty a mysterious archetypal foreknowledge of the direction we as a society must travel to reach our highest good. The double termination of these crystals permits us to move back and forth in history to unravel the mystery challenge of the great myths.

All the great myths are a culture's dream—the collective, subconscious prophecy of an entire people. Interpreting the meaning of the great myths is as important to us, as a people, as understanding our dreams is to us as individuals. If we do not look into the mythic prophecies and learn from their deep wisdom, we will stay stuck, as a society and on the personal level, right where the archetypal symbols end in the myth.

A Mythic Crystal can be programmed and inspired to hold within itself whatever mythic prophecy we ask. If you would like to help society and yourself work out a mythic mystery, simply tell the story of the myth to your crystal, and then ask it to resolve that myth.

You can do this with any myth you choose, especially those myths that seem critical for our times. For instance, the story of Robin Hood speaks of a desire for social justice, just as the myth of Avalon expresses our longing to restore a mystical worldview and to renew humankind's respect for women and feminine attributes.

Let us assume here that you have asked a Mythic Crystal to work out the Avalon mystery. The Mythic Crystal then becomes an Avalon Crystal and will remain so until our society works out this prophecy. It will always be an Avalon until that time.

The end of the perfection of Camelot and the subsequent disappearance of the magical isle of Avalon into the mists symbolize the defeat of the primal people who lived close to nature and revered the feminine principal as equal to the male. As these Nature People were hounded and destroyed, our modern civilization arose, where all the qualities seen as feminine were viewed as either evil or worthless: emotions, gentleness, sensuality, softness, dreaminess, creativity and non-hierarchical spirituality divorced from major institutions. But you can't kill these things. You can only drive them into hiding for a while. So all the beauty of Camelot, all the qualities that make life worth living, retreated to an island hidden by mist, the island of Avalon. And they retreated to our subconscious minds to be unveiled and seen by those who understand that mystery, magic, emotions, spontaneity and sensuality are not to be run away from but are to be embraced as part of the great wheel of life.

An Avalon Crystal can help us retrieve the hidden, female part of ourselves, whether we are male or female, and can lift the veil of the magical isle of Avalon once again.

Avalons Speak:

You'll find them not so far away,
Merlin and Arthur and Morgyn La Fey.
Enshrouded in mist, enclouded in haze,
The magical, beautiful ancient ways
Of walking in balance upon the green earth,
Respecting the mother and giving her worth.

When fear of the feminine spirit is gone,
We will all return from Avalon.

PARITY CRYSTALS

Any cluster of identically-sized crystals is an egalitarian or Parity Crystal. These crystals teach us to wean ourselves from authority figures of all kinds. Parities show us that we are all peers on a spiritual level, and that the spirit realm is open to all alike. Parity Crystals awaken within us the knowledge that we all make up the sacred circle of life, and each of us has something important to contribute in our growth towards the light.

The human race is evolving away from needing spiritual hierarchy. A Parity Crystal encourages us to look within for our spiritual answers rather than relying on outer authority. Further, it enables us to trust the answers received from our own deep wisdom. Parities teach us that every living being has truth and wisdom to impart but that no single person has the whole answer. We all need to share and to contribute our portion of the light, for together we are the answer.

Parities Speak:

Born equal in wisdom, equal in soul,
Together we're the circle, together we're the whole.

Equal in the spirit, all children of the light,
Our selves are all the greater, when our selves unite.

PHANTOM CRYSTALS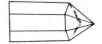

Within a Phantom Crystal is another crystal or the dim outline of another crystal. This phenomenon results when a crystal stops growing for awhile and then resumes its growth again.

Phantom Crystals are excellent for helping us gain awareness of our past lives and our future incarnations as well. They are also helpers in all kinds of inner growth, encouraging us to extend beyond our current limitations. They teach us to transcend the limiting mindsets we might have and to reach beyond the mundane, the expected and the typical in all we do.

Phantoms also remind us of the reality of life after death. For when the growing time on this Earth plane is over, we stop momentarily, only to develop into another incarnation on this or some other plane. Phantoms teach us that death is not something to be feared but is just a little rest before we grow again in ways more beautiful than before.

PIXILATED (ENCHANTED) CRYSTALS

A Double Terminated Crystal with a rainbow inside, as well as a lot of faerie frost within it, is a Pixilated or Enchanted Crystal. These crystals have the ability to awaken us to the beauty, the delight, the wonder of our world. They open the door to a world of enchantment right here on Earth. An Enchanted Crystal opens our eyes to all the numinous beings who share the earth plane with us: unicorns, dragons, naiads, plant and animal devas, elemental spirits and so forth.

Once you become enchanted by one of these crystals, you become pixilated. And then a wonderful world opens up to you, right in your own backyard. You can walk outside and meet Pan, the woodland god, hear him playing his flute and feel his lusty, life-loving energy all around you. You can see and speak to all the so-called mythical beings who live on the Earth concurrently with humans but in a form invisible to mundane people—those who have not been enchanted.

Take an Enchanted Crystal to a quiet, natural place.

Spiritual Values of Crystals

Standing still, breathe deeply and let your heart be filled with the wonder and beauty of nature. Then wave the crystal around yourself in great arcs. You may be moved to dance or sing as you do this. At any rate, feel yourself connected in the celebration of life with the trees, the grass, the air, the earth. Ask aloud to be enchanted, to be touched, to be inspired, to be captivated, charmed, delighted and fascinated by all the beings of and on the Earth.

Enchanted Crystals Speak:

The Pan pipes of nature entice you away
From a worldview that's cold, that is drab
*   and is gray*

To a world filled with wonder and beauty and grace,
To a glittering, sparkling, magical place.

The dragons, the naiads, the unicorns all
Invite you, entreat you to heed their fey call.

Earth is more than a place to endure, to survive —
It is sacred, enchanted, sublimely alive!

QUANTUM CRYSTALS

When three or more Double-Terminated crystals join together, they become a Quantum Crystal. The new physics tells us that reality is constantly being created and altered on many planes simultaneously; that, indeed, there is no such thing as the hard and fast reality our limited senses perceive but simply endless probability waves.

Just before a probability wave collapses and a new

world is born (or some aspect of what we perceive of as reality manifests) there is a gap, a breath, a moment in which our prayers, thoughts, wishes and desires can influence the probable outcome.

To alter the statistical probabilities of your wish coming true, you might hold a Quantum Crystal in your hands, state your wish or prayer and ask that a probability wave collapses in your favor. To put it in a simpler way, Quantums are good crystals to pray with.

Quantums Speak:

I am the pause, I am the ebb,
Linking together all the world's web.

Exploring alternatives, endless and deep,
As consciousness takes a quantum leap

The space between stars, the blink of an eye,
As worlds are born and others die

And with a wish are born anew,
And the world and the wish—the Creator—is you!

RAINBOW CRYSTALS

If you turn a crystal this way and that in bright light, you may see a rainbow inside. Such crystals are considered helpful for promoting feelings of hope, happiness and optimism. They are also good at letting us see the endlessly beautiful potential of the universe—and of our own lives.

Spiritual Values of Crystals

Rainbow Crystals can awaken us especially to the beauty of nature. They bring us the realization that although we live again and again on many different planes of reality, there is only one earth plane. And Earth is both beautiful and unique. While we are manifest here, the Rainbows teach us, we must drink in Earth's wonder and magic. For the sun on our bodies, the moon on the water, the wind in our hair are blessings bestowed on us for but a brief span. Rainbow Crystals induce us, invite us, to leave our man-made houses and go outside to our Creator-made home. They teach us that we have paradise right here on Earth, if only we'll notice.

Rainbow Crystals show us that when we attune ourselves to Mother Nature, our lives become whole. A human life devoid of contact with nature cannot be a satisfying life, for we were incarnated on Earth for many reasons. And chief among those reasons is our capacity to celebrate, enjoy, respect, befriend, protect and revere our sacred Earth Mother.

RECEIVING CRYSTALS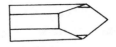

Having one broad flat face, these crystals are considered good for drawing or receiving energy. Therefore, many healers put the flat face against a body part that is ailing to draw out the negative energy. People also put a Receiving Crystal to their heart or head to draw out any negative thoughts or feelings. Others will hold a Receiving Crystal in one hand (often the left hand, which is considered the receptive hand) and a Projecting Crystal in the right hand simultaneously to receive and give a specific energy that they call upon: For instance, in working with a healing energy, they might visualize white light entering the Receiving Crystal. They would then visualize this light passing through their body (which acts as a conductor) and flowing out the Projecting Crystal toward whichever individual or situation the healing energy is intended for.

Receiving Crystals also help us to become more receptive, to take in the good and the pleasurable, to accept and assimilate new concepts and to accept people nonjudgmentally.

RIGHT-HANDED CRYSTALS

Right-Handed Crystals have an extra facet on the right side of the largest facet of the crystal. These crystals are considered to be dynamic, projective and energizing when held in the right hand, which is the active side of the body.

Right-Handed Crystals activate the left hemisphere of the brain, which is logical, intellectual and action-oriented. Therefore, this crystal promotes rationality and reasonableness and is thought to aid in any endeavor calling for analytical ability and intellectual acuity.

This crystal is said to encourage study and learning. It therefore proves a good companion during any intellectual pursuit.

ROSE QUARTZ

Gemstone lore considers Rose Quartz as the most loving of stones, indeed, as one of the most loving beings on this planet. She enhances all forms of love: self-love, mother love, caring, kindness, platonic and romantic love. This gentle yet powerful stone is all "heart," opening the hearts of those who befriend her with her tender, peaceful and comforting energy.

For those of us who did not receive unconditional love as children, Rose Quartz emanates that kind of nurturance. When it is worn near the heart, this stone can infuse its wearer with healing, mothering love. As the heart is filled with this healing solace, that person can then let their love flow out to others and to themselves as well.

Rose Quartz will also help us attract positive, gentle, nurturing love into our lives. Hold a Rose Quartz over your heart each night as you lie in bed, ready for sleep. Pray for love. Pray to attract loving people into your life and be more loving in return. She is the mothering stone, who teaches us to be more forgiving and tolerant by bathing us in her tender love.

Rose Quartz Speaks:

Gentle and kind, loving and tender,
I am soul's ease and the heart's mender.
Soft as a doe, pure as a dove,
I bathe your heart in healing love
So that in your turn you might
Bathe all life with love's warm light.

Crystal Wisdom

RUTILATED QUARTZ CRYSTALS

Rutilated Quartz promotes determination, self-control and strength of will. This is a stone of high resolve, assisting our own strength of mind and self-reliance. Whenever we have a goal that must be accomplished, Rutilated Quartz is of great help, as it increases volition. Steadfastness and firmness are this stone's great gifts to all those who work with him. Hold him to your solar plexus, the seat of the will, and breathe deeply. Feel your will becoming strong and filled with light.

For those who have trouble making decisions or are too easily led by others, Rutilated Quartz has been found to be very helpful because it teaches us moral courage and grants us the resolve to stride forward in life with intention and purpose. This stone furthermore encourages us to hold on to our positive, life-affirming convictions while going after our dreams with determination and tenacity.

SELENE CRYSTALS

A crystal with any rounded inclusion is attuned to lunar energies and is therefore called a Selene Crystal. It is more common to find a half or three-quarter moon than a full moon inside a crystal, but any rounded shape within makes it a Selene. Selene Crystals promote psychic ability, gentleness, insight into the mysteries and all the qualities we think of as feminine.

Selene is the Moon Goddess: her namesake crystal

expresses her abilities in conjunction with the moon's phases.

During the new moon, you might place a Selene Crystal in direct moonlight. She will then be filled with the energies of hope, youth and new beginnings. Carry her with you and she will reflect these qualities back to you. Because the new moon is also a time to begin new projects and to plant positive ideas in the subconscious mind, a Selene Crystal is best programmed and inspired for these qualities at this time.

Since the full moon is the time for fulfillment of wishes, dreams and desires, this is the asking time, the time when the wide realm of possibility pours forth upon those who wish and pray. You might place a Selene Crystal under the full moon so that she will be infused with the energies of abundance, nurturance, generosity, fulfillment and love.

Selene Crystals Speak:

Priestess am I to the goddess Selene,
Protectress of life and the night's silver Queen,
Reflecting so softly, so sweetly above
The gentle abundance of feminine love.

Hold me so near to receive, to attune,
The light of my lady, Selene, the moon.

SEVEN-FACETED CRYSTALS

A Seven-Faceted Crystal enhances truthfulness, serenity, harmony and cosmic consciousness. This is a very intuitive and inspirational crystal. It is recognized for its balancing properties and is considered effective for inducing a quiet, introspective, calming energy upon those who keep it near. Therefore, a Seven-Faceted Crystal is an excellent stone to place in a turbulent atmosphere or to use in conjunction with any situation or person in turmoil. Seven-Faceted Crystals are the quiet philosophers of the quartz clan. Their gentle mysticism and spiritual attainment bestow a transcendent peace upon all who befriend them.

SMOKY QUARTZ

Gemstone lore considers Smoky Quartz to promote serenity, calmness and positive thoughts. It is thought helpful in calming fears, soothing nerves and lifting depression. It is a stabilizing, grounding stone, encouraging a mindset that is practical and rooted in reality while at the same time spiritual. Because of this, it is a good stone to befriend if you tend to be too ethereal and need to tap more grounding energy without losing your transcendent perspective as you become more practical and earthbound.

Smoky Quartz can help us turn our wishes, dreams and desires into reality. This lovely quartz ranges in color from dark gray to black and is linked to the subconscious mind. Therefore, it is a good friend to keep with us whenever we need to tap the wisdom of the collective subconscious, which is all the minds of the world linked at a subconscious level. There is great wisdom and power in the unconscious, and Smoky Quartz can help it unfold.

Spiritual Values of Crystals

Smoky is the zen master of the stones, teaching us to simplify our lives and carry out life's details in a centered, spiritual manner. Smoky teaches us to live our daily life in a sacred manner and to take a zen approach to life. If we infuse even the smallest details of our lives with meaning, spirit and awareness, then our entire lives will be a balance between the sacred spirit plane and the sacred earth plane.

Smoky Quartz Speaks:

I am the beauty in practical things.
While stirring the oatmeal, the spirit still sings.

While tilling the soil, the heart can still love;
For as is below, so is above.

When you make the mundane a deep meditation,
The daily routine becomes spirit's elation.

SOULMATE CRYSTALS

Two crystals attached side by side, of a similar size, are Soulmate Crystals. (They are also known as Twin Crystals). This unifying stone promotes loving contact, tender communication and togetherness.

On a personal level, a Soulmate Crystal helps us to find and then to merge with a kindred spirit with whom we have traveled eternally through many incarnations on Earth and on other planes. A soulmate is a person in eternal kinship with your innermost self.

To locate your soulmate, you might sleep with a Soulmate Crystal each night. As you fall asleep, pray with the crystal that you find a kindred spirit on this Earth, in this life. In fact, you can speak into the Soulmate Crystal and your heart's call will be transmitted to the subconscious of your soulmate and will act as a signal beam to guide that person to you. When you and your soulmate have united, each of you might wear a Soulmate Crystal to strengthen your connection, intimacy and mutuality.

On a spiritual level, Soulmate Crystals teach us to blend with all life and to realize that our soul is wed in eternal kinship with all sentient beings.

Soulmate Crystals Speak:

Through daylight and darkness and worlds
*   without end*
You've travelled together, you and your friend.

In one life, kin; in another life, wed;
Sometimes the leader, sometimes the led,

Incarnate on other planets than Earth,
Together in death, together in birth.

It is I who will guide you once again
And help you find your cosmic friend.

Call through me, pray through me; it is my goal
To help you meet your kindred soul.

SPIRIT GUARDIAN CRYSTALS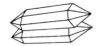

A double terminated Soulmate Crystal helps us contact our spirit guardians. Our spirit guardians have traveled with us through many incarnations, but they are currently dwelling on the spirit plane. They may be human, plant, animal or mineral; and you may have more than one. For example, my spirit guardians are an angel, a Bear Spirit and an Oak Tree Spirit.

Our spirit guardians protect and guide us. A Spirit Guardian Crystal helps us contact them.

Again, it is as simple as praying through a Spirit Guardian Crystal to contact your spirit friends. They are with you at all times, whether you know it or not. They are awaiting the time you invite them to make conscious contact. You may be surprised how quickly communication can be established through this crystal. Just ask for help or guidance in anything and be receptive to "hearing" their answer in your heart, your visualizations, your feelings or your mind—or by some sychronicity or sign as you go through your daily life.

TABULAR CRYSTALS

Tabular Crystals have a flattened shape. Common crystal lore attributes to Tabulars the power to enhance communication, integration, smooth energy flow and balance.

All quartz crystals facilitate communication, but Tabulars are the communication experts of the quartz clan. They promote any positive exchange of energies between conscious beings. Tabular crystals facilitate understanding and dialogue between people, and they also help us communicate with nature and with spirit beings as well.

Tabulars foster an exciting and stimulating interchange between differing clans, species and minds. They also help us to bridge the communication gap between our own hearts and minds, thus enabling us to translate feelings into verbal communication or mental awareness.

Any form of communication is strengthened in the presence of a Tabular Crystal.

TEACHING SPIRIT CRYSTALS

If you turn a quartz crystal this way or that you may see the shape of a being inside it. This is the teaching spirit within the crystal. It may be a human, animal or plant which was once an incarnate being on Earth and lived a life of such purity and wisdom that it was allowed to reincarnate into a crystal. This is a great teacher spirit, and you can get guidance and help from this being. Some crystals have more than one teacher within them. A crystal teaching spirit can become a close personal friend and has specifically chosen you to guide and work with.

It's possible to have a crystal with you for years without discovering the teaching spirit that dwells in it. Nevertheless, when you become receptive to that spirit's wisdom, it will inevitably reveal itself to you.

TWIN FLAME CRYSTALS

Twin Flames are two crystals of a similar size joined at the base and then flared out in a v shape. Twin Flames share similar energies with Soulmate Crystals. They foster cooperation, union, togetherness and fusion. But Twin Flame Crystals specifically help us attract our spiritual partners. These are not necessarily people we will mate with; these are, rather, people who will work with us and be our life's companions in the spirit. With our twin flame we will grow together and walk together to our highest good on our highest path, for ours is the same path. Our twin flame is our spiritual mate in our eternal journey through vast time and space—a cosmic friend.

Once a person finds his or her soulmate, it eventually dawns on them that there's someone else out there. They need their soulmate, and yet they need their twin flame also. (On rare occasions a soulmate is also a twin flame.) At any rate, a Twin Flame Crystal kept with you at all times will help you attract your spiritual life partner.

Twin Flame Crystals Speak:

Not a love, nor a mate,
But an even higher fate
Unites yourself with your Twin Flame,
Separate souls and yet the same.

Ever one, yet ever free—
Converging for eternity.

Together, spirits rise and soar
Where one soul could not go before.

99

WAND CRYSTALS

A slender crystal at least three and a half inches long is a Wand. Wands are distinguished from Artemis Crystals by size; a Wand Crystal is much longer and somewhat wider. These are the magic wands that the wizards, high priestesses and magicians of old used. Sometimes they would attach these crystals to a straight tree branch, to tap into Tree Spirit energy as well as crystal power.

When held in the hand, these crystals extend our manifestation powers greatly. When you wave a Wand Crystal around and make a wish or even make a statement, you are actually working very powerful magic. It is therefore most important to act responsibly when working with a Wand Crystal. Never point a Wand Crystal at anyone in jest, and never say or wish for anything negative when working with a Wand. And ask only for that which is positive and life-affirming because all energy that is projected through a Wand Crystal returns to the sender in magnified form. Send good, healing energy out, and you will receive that which you send tenfold. Wands are a great gift, given to us by our Earth Mother, to be used wisely. When you experience for yourself a Wand's power, you will automatically treat this great gift with the respect it deserves.

The most common way to work with a Wand Crystal is to stand with your legs slightly apart. Breathe deeply until you are calm and centered, then pick up your Wand. Hold it at the base, pointing it outward to the universe. Then state your prayer or visualize your intent, while waving the Wand clockwise in a circle. (Clockwise, or sunwise, is considered the direction of increasing energy.)

Wands are also used for protection, most often by drawing an imaginary circle around yourself, your house or whatever you want to protect with the Wand. As you do this you might visualize white light coming out of the point of the crystal. Be sure to travel or move the Wand in a clockwise direction. You might also speak some heartfelt words of protection and shielding as you do this, or you might chant this protection prayer: "I (or this house) am ever protected by the Light. Only good can come to me. Only good can flow from me. Only good can be here. I am ever protected by the Light."

Wands are sometimes thought of as psychic knives, and some people use them symbolically to cut away negative psychological, emotional or psychic patterns. (Remember, this is symbolic. You do not physically cut anything with a Wand.) I feel strongly that it is best to work with Wands in positive terms, especially if you are just starting out with them. In other words, instead of "cutting away" whatever you might perceive as negative, it is more effective to use the Wand to manifest a positive alternative.

Whenever you work with any crystal, it is best to focus on the positive rather than try to banish the negative. Crystals and our own higher selves are more responsive to positive statements. For example, "I affirm abundance and prosperity for myself and for all beings" will resonate better with the spirit realm than "I am not and will never be poor again." The subconscious mind has a hard time recognizing negatives. The second sentence might come through as "I am poor and will be poor again." So state everything positively!

101

WINDOW CRYSTALS

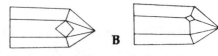

Window Crystals have an extra diamond-shaped facet. Although some people feel that the diamond-shaped "window" must be a certain size and in a specific position (see diagram A), I have found that any diamond-shaped facet on a crystal is a Window Crystal.

A large and symmetrically shaped window will let us see the better known spirit worlds, such as the realms of angels and spirit guardians. But the oddly positioned, smaller windows lead us to worlds that are either harder to reach from a corporeal, earthplane existence or are simply less well known, such as the realms of extra-terrestrials, devas and goddesses. These Window Crystals can also guide us to a parallel existence, where our lives are being led on an Earth that is a paradise. Through such Window Crystals, we can visit that paradise and return with a clearer vision of what our lives can be like if we work towards positive transformation.

Just as small, asymmetrical Window Crystals lead us to alternative spirit planes, so do they guide us to alternate mundane realities and mindsets. We find, when we keep such Window Crystals near us, that we begin to have more choices open to us. We suddenly become aware of how many varied and beautiful options are ours in how we live our lives and what we choose to hold in our consciousness.

All Window Crystals offer us the great gift of communication with our own souls or spirits, which is important in helping us gain an expanded perspective on our lives. Our egos, our personalities, are finite. But within each of us there is a higher, eternal self. To the extent that we can communicate with this part of ourselves we can receive great wisdom, comfort, and guidance. We can conduct our lives from a more cosmic orientation.

If the window on the crystal is large enough to gaze into, you can work with these mind and spirit openers in that way. If the window is tiny, you might hold it to your third eye or place the window over your heart. However, just keeping a Window Crystal nearby will also have a beneficial effect.

Window Crystals Speak:

Hold me gently in your hand;
A window to another land,
A different time, a world afar,
A journey to a distant star.

Hold me again, as at the start;
Now find that same place in your heart.

WORLDLY CRYSTALS

Worldly Crystals are those that help us in the mundane world. They are the crystals in watches, lasers, computers and various electronic circuitry. As you go through your daily life, you can interact with these crystals to good effect. For instance, there are silicon chips in the checkout machine at your local supermarket. You can, while standing in line, send a positive visualization or thought form into those crystals, programming or inspiring them to help provide enough food for everyone on Earth. Or when you are standing in line at the bank, you can send a thought form to all the silicon chips (crystals) in the bank computers to bring prosperity to all beings. In universities and educational institutions you can mentally inspire all the silicon chips in the computers to facilitate worldwide wisdom, and so forth.

Worldly Crystals teach us that a serene and hopeful mindset can be attained in the middle of the busy work-a-day world. We need not wait for a specific time or location to express our meditative, affirmative selves. Spirituality can shine forth everywhere we go and in everything we do.

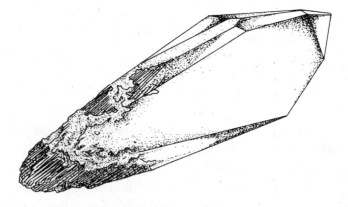

CHAPTER V
SPIRITUAL VALUES
OF GEMSTONES

AGATE - *Agate comes in a broad range of colors and is often variegated and banded. It is a member of the quartz family.*

Gemstone Lore: According to conventional wisdom, Agates enhance love, abundance, wealth, good luck, longevity, harmony, courage, protection and truthfulness. Agates are very powerful stones. They help us become balanced and harmonious in body, mind and spirit because they are themselves an expression of the wholeness and balance of nature. A most earth-loving stone, the Agate expresses the life-affirming abundance and protectiveness of Earth Mother. Therefore Agates are traditionally considered to bring protection and abundance to all who wear them.

Crystal Wisdom

Agates teach us to be more generous and also help us to overcome bitterness of the heart and inner anger. Furthermore, Agate has been thought of as a stone that attracts love; for as it clears away the bitterness of negativity in our hearts, it opens us up to the love and sweetness around us. When we become more loving, we then attract love into our lives.

In addition to the powers common to all Agates, these particular types of Agates have their own attributes as well. BOTSWANA AGATE: Fertility, sensuality, artistic expression, comfort. DENDRITIC AGATE: Safe travel, loyalty, tranquility. FERN AGATE: Helps us communicate with plants. FIRE AGATE: Courage, enthusiasm. IRIS AGATE: Honor, joy, popularity, longevity. LACE AGATE: See page 162. MOSS AGATE: See page 137. PLUME AGATE: Enhances imagination and visualization.

Agate Speaks:

Those who befriend me know and see
The Earth in her entirety.

Healing and wise, protective and strong,
I sing to you a loving song.

A tiny Earth Mother in your hand ,
Expression of Air, Fire, Water and Land,

My charge always has been and always will be:
Heal the Earth, as I heal thee!

Spiritual Values of Gemstones

AMAZONITE - *Amazonite is a green member of the feldspar clan.*

Gemstone Lore: Traditional wisdom holds that Amazonite bestows truth, sincerity and honor; a stone of communication, she improves eloquence, allowing us to "speak from the heart." Amazonite's impeccable energy encourages honesty and integrity in all situations. She promotes candor, openness, truth and trust, at the same time teaching us to see with clear sight and expanded vision. For she is a prophetess of the mineral clan. When held to the third eye (the forehead), Amazonite unlocks the "starlight vision," the ability to see the past, present and future with depth and clarity. She fosters clairvoyant visions, for she can see far and deep; and that which she sees, she relates with courage and insight. As she speaks truth and teaches us to do likewise, Amazonite is very useful for divination and prophecy of all kinds, making an excellent companion when doing Tarot, I Ching and so forth.

Amazonite is the patron stone of those who wish to develop their clairvoyant abilities.

Amazonite Speaks:

You hold in your hands a tiny truthseeker,
A seer of visions, an eloquent speaker.
And all that I see, I truly impart
Straight from the spirit and right from the heart,
To serve the Truth, to foster the Light.
I am the stone you call Amazonite.

107

AMBER - *Amber is solidified and petrified sap from a pine tree. Its color is golden or amber.*

Gemstone Lore: Amber is traditionally said to bring romantic love, purification and wisdom. Amber is also recognized for its energizing, healing and balancing properties and is considered effective for lifting depression. Amber imbues those who befriend it with the ageless wisdom of the pine trees. Ancient and wise, patient and strong, the attributes of the pines are condensed in this lovely golden being.

Lady Amber is a gentle stone who helps its wearer to become calm and mellow. She not only draws out negative energy from the body but generally purifies the spirit and heart as well. Kept in the house or office, Amber can cleanse the atmosphere of negative vibrations. Finally, because Amber helps preserve ancient wisdom and knowledge, it is excellent for rediscovering our previous lives on Earth through dreams and meditations. Amber also helps us unfold the great knowledge of Atlantis and of all the old, wise peoples of the Earth.

Amber Speaks:

Lifeblood of an ancient pine,
Knowledge and wisdom and truth are mine.

A Spirit Pine, glowing gold,
I sing of the love and wisdom of old.

Hold me closely to your heart,
And all I know, I will impart.

AMETHYST - See page 56.

Spiritual Values of Gemstones

APATITE - *Apatite comes in a variety of colors ranging from yellow to green, white, brown or light purple.*

Gemstone Lore: Apatite, according to conventional understanding, fosters communication, concentration, clarity of thought and intellect. In that Apatite is considered to help focus our minds and improve concentration, it stands us in good stead whenever we want to speak or write clearly and eloquently. Basically, it is very useful in all intellectual pursuits, thanks to its help in developing our conceptual and logical abilities.

Apatite's strength and wisdom is the ability to foster peace and harmony through communication. He is a gemstone of great understanding and perception, stimulating our minds and hearts towards a continual interchange of thoughts and ideas between people. In addition, Apatite helps us to communicate with nature, with the spirit plane and with our own subconscious as well.

AQUAMARINE - *Aquamarine is a blue-green member of the beryl clan.*

Gemstone Lore: This stone is associated with the calming effect of the sea and is traditionally used to soothe, calm and alleviate fears and phobias. It aids in cleansing, meditation and appreciation of nature. It brings serenity and peace to those who keep it near.

Aquamarine's attributes are attuned to the ocean, and the sea's cleansing, soothing effect can be found in this stone. A wise grandmother of the mineral clan, she opens us to oceanic consciousness, grants tranquility and ease and helps us get in touch with the Nature Spirits of the sea.

Aquamarine helps us communicate with all sea life

and connects us to the ocean, even if we live far from it. She will also influence us to protect ocean life and appreciate all the wise and beautiful dwellers in the sea.

Hold her in your hand as you close your eyes and visualize the dolphins. Ask for a message of wisdom from them; then still your mind and await an answer . . . Now send healing energy through the stone, to the dolphins . . . Visualize the oceans and all the waters of the earth running clean and clear again.

Aquamarine Speaks:

You hold in your hands the spirit of ocean,
Teaching you calmness, peace and devotion.

I am the seawomb, of all life the start;
I offer you comfort and peace of the heart.

Call me grandmother; in me be serene.
I am the stone you call Aquamarine.

AVENTURINE - *Ranging in color from golden brown to green, Aventurine is a member of the quartz clan.*

Gemstone Lore: Long associated with creativity, imagination, prosperity, career success and balance, Aventurine opens us up to the world of opportunities. It helps us see potentials and alternatives in the mundane, practical side of life and in the more spiritual side as well. On a wordly level, when we can better perceive all the potentials a given situation has to offer, we can increase our opportunities for career growth and prosperity. On a higher level, when we see many alternatives, we become more adept at tapping our unique creative flow.

Green Aventurine is considered especially healing of body, mind and spirit. Furthermore, it has a calming and soothing effect on those who wear it.

AZURITE - *Azurite is a blue, metallic mineral.*

Gemstone Lore: Traditional wisdom holds that Azurite promotes clear understanding, cleansing, healing, perspective, purification, patience, kindness, prophecy and truth. It is regarded as a stone that can help make the subconscious more available to the conscious and unite heavenly energy with earthly pursuits. It also offers spiritual guidance and promotes psychic dreams.

Azurite's essence is of the sky. It expands the limits of our minds, opening us to the all. From this awareness comes understanding, a clearer perspective and new ways of looking at things. Because Azurite helps bring the spiritual into the mundane, it can help us see all life on Earth as sacred.

It is traditionally considered a very strong and powerful healer and is the shaman, or high priest, of the mineral clan, whose abilities range well beyond the limits we think of as "normal". Azurite brings energy to New Age ideas and, in a wise and caring way, nurtures the revolutionary thinking that can transform the world to the highest good. Yet at the same time he knows and follows primordial healing practices. He can combine the heavenly and the earthly in a sacred, balanced way and impart this knowledge to us. Azurite teaches us and guides us in all he knows, and his knowledge is as vast and broad as the sky he manifests.

Azurite Speaks:

Wide and blue as the open sky,
I teach your spirit to soar, to fly
To lands that are new, to lands that are old,
So that your shamanic powers unfold.

Journey with me to the spirit world,
Then return to earth with wings unfurled!

BLACK OBSIDIAN - *Black Obsidian is formed when lava is quickly cooled.*

Gemstone Lore: Black Obsidian is a powerful stone dedicated to change, transformation, metamorphosis, purification, fulfillment, inner growth and introspection. He is linked with the physical plane and, as such, exerts a grounding energy upon those around him. Black Obsidian develops practicality and pragmatism, teaching us to get in touch with reality, to strip ourselves of illusions and to deal with the earth plane effectively. Yet he also appreciates the mystery of the psychic plane, knowing full well that it is good to walk in both the realms of spirit and the realms of mundane reality, to be successful in both worlds. In fact, Black Obsidian teaches us that the earth plane is the place to start with; for if you cannot master that, you cannot be adroit in other, more numinous planes. A teaching stone, who exposes our rationalizations and illusions about ourselves, Black Obsidian encourages us to face our faults in order to correct them.

He is thought of as a very powerful stone, representing night at its darkest—a sphere filled with mystery yet blanketed in peace, inducing deep magical dreams and intuitive wisdom. To some, the blackness of night is frightening, especially to those who fear their own subconscious impulses and motivations. Black Obsidian gets us in touch with those parts of ourselves we consciously keep hidden. Though buried deep within the darkness along with our secrets and fears, they are nevertheless transformed into precious jewels when they are brought to the light of awareness.

GOLDEN OBSIDIAN increases self-control and is useful for habit-breaking. MAHOGANY OBSIDIAN promotes acceptance of our sensuality, and SNOW-FLAKE OBSIDIAN keeps us balanced during times of change.

Black Obsidian Speaks:

You hold in your hands the secret of night;
I grant inner vision's intuitive sight.

I teach you to face your darkest fears,
To learn from laughter a well as from tears.

For buried deep within is your power—
Face it, and own it so that it may flower!

BLOODSTONE - *This quartz family member is dark green, with red flecks.*
Gemstone Lore: Traditional teachings consider the Bloodstone to enhance alignment, organization and smooth energy flow. It is also said to bring rain, abundance, generosity, idealism and good fortune. Usually thought of as the great purifier, it is considered able to remove emotional and physical blockages.

It is good to keep a Bloodstone in any place that needs its energy cleansed. When first moving into a dwelling place, for instance, many people place a Bloodstone in a central spot and pray with the stone for a cleansing and purification of energies in that home. It will help purify the mind as well as the body and spirit. Those who are troubled by negative thoughts might place a small Bloodstone on the forehead , while lying down. They will then find it easier to turn the mind to positive affirmations and thoughts.

CALCITE - *Calcite is the most common carbonate mineral. Colors range from opaque to brown, green, orange and gold.*

Gemstone Lore: According to conventional understanding, Calcite is attuned to the mental plane. GOLD CALCITE is said to deepen intellect, wisdom, psychic abilities, channeling and higher consciousness. GREEN CALCITE is known as a healer on the mental plane, aiding mental balance, helping us release old and limiting ideas and facilitating communication between the head and the heart. CLEAR CALCITE (also known as Iceland Spar) fosters spirituality. GRAY CALCITE encourages calmness and serenity. RED CALCITE opens the heart chakra.

Calcite is also regarded as a strengthener in times of mental anguish and turmoil, and as a helper in the transition to new ideas. As a stone of the mind, Calcite is a helpful companion to have during any intellectual pursuit. It is commonly used as a study partner, and is especially good as a channel to higher forces. A wise and balancing stone, Calcite imbues all those near it with wisdom and mental harmony.

CARNELIAN - *Carnelian is a form of chalcedony, and is a member of the quartz family. Its color is reddish-orange or brown.*

Gemstone lore emphasizes Carnelian's power to enhance energy flow, creativity, individuality, past life recall, emotional warmth, sociability, courage, happiness, self-esteem, rebirth and memory.

Carnelian's red-orange and sometimes brown coloring is the very essence of autumn, the harvest time. And, as Carnelian is a harvester of dreams, it is good to hold a Carnelian in your hand and make a wish to harvest something you have worked hard for.

A relative of the Agate, Carnelian is an earth-oriented, nature-loving stone. He teaches us to come into harmony with the laws of nature and with the turning of the seasons. Carnelian leads us to revere the Earth, attuning ourselves to the elements and seasons, so that our lives can be further harmonized. He teaches us that the apparent death autumn brings is but an illusion; for the great wheel of Earth Mother turns, and once again comes spring and rebirth. Likewise, Carnelian calms our fears about death and rebirth and allows us to see our past lives, reassuring us that life does not end but circles endlessly—like the seasons themselves.

Carnelian Speaks:

Harvest your wishes, harvest your dreams,
Gather in stardust, reap the mooon's beams.

All things are possible—but love the Earth first!
She feeds your hunger, she quenches your thirst.

115

Life never ending, of autumn I sing.
Yes, winter cometh, but comes then the spring.

I sing of the seasons, Earth Mother's great wheel.
Attune to the rhythm to harvest and heal.

CELESTITE - *Celestite is light blue or white.*

Gemstone Lore: Celestite augments spiritual development, enlightenment, awareness and candor. This is a most spiritual stone, allowing us to get closer to our Creator. Celestite encourages and facilitates prayer and teaches us to live our spirituality day by day in quiet, kind, empathic contact with all beings.

This stone helps us to broaden our outlook and widen our perspective. He is a stone that teaches us to be open, frank, straightforward, simple and innocent; for he embodies clarity of thought and pureness of heart. Celestite is attuned to celestial energy. He promotes communication with the heavenly realms, with the angels and seraphs. Because Celestite also helps us to contact our guardian angels, you might place this spiritual stone under your pillow at night and pray, as you are falling asleep, to be visited by your own guardian angel. Some people find that their angel offers advice and loving guidance through the dream state. Others actually have an angelic visitation.

Celestite is the patron stone of those who seek spiritual enlightenment.

CHALCEDONY - *This quartz can be white or bluish but is usually gray.*

Gemstone Lore: Chalcedony is regarded as a stone

that augments vitality, stamina and endurance. This powerful stone has an energizing effect on people and situations. With vigorous intensity and life-loving hardiness, Chalcedony imparts a hale and robust glow upon all who befriend her. Under the warm influence of her mothering and nurturing aura, people, pets and projects flourish and grow. Generosity of soul and expansiveness of heart are the gifts of this jovial and loving stone. She is a great, abundant motherstone of the mineral clan. It is she who knows and teaches that the more we give, the more we receive. And she imparts her knowledge with a spirited, vibrant energy, enlivening all who come to know and love her.

And yet there is a soft and tender side to this great motherstone, for she also promotes kindness, charity, friendliness and a feeling of oneness and equality with all life.

CHRYSOBERYL - *This stone ranges in color from yellow to green.*

Gemstone Lore: Tradition has it that Chrysoberyl builds kindness, generosity, forgiveness and benevolence. Emotionally uplifting, this stone imparts hope, optimism and energy to all new projects and relationships. Because Chrysoberyl is dedicated to new beginnings, it is very protective to all young life. This stone suggests the essence of springtime, of youth and of innocence. For this reason, it is considered a restorative and energizer.

Those who keep it near often find that they become more forgiving and understanding, for this is also a very compassionate stone.

Crystal Wisdom

CHRYSOCOLLA - *The color is blue, green or both.*

Gemstone Lore: Chrysocolla is linked with tranquility, serenity, and peace. She represents the water element as manifested in clear, calm bodies of water such as lakes and ponds. This stone embodies the feminine energies of soft, quiet strength and deep subconscious wisdom. Therefore, Chrysocolla can help us get in touch with our own subconscious intuitions and motivations as well as linking us with the life-affirming genius of the collective subconscious. Chrysocolla fosters patience, nurturance, acceptance and tolerance. She radiates supportive, unconditional love to all who befriend her. A stone of profound depth and stillness, she calms the emotions and soothes the soul. Hers is a pensive, thoughtful energy, lending great help and inspiration to those who meditate and seek the "still, small voice within." Yet Chrysocolla is also associated with hope, a sense of wonder and an appreciation for mystery. This stone is also excellent at promoting intimacy and so is good to keep at hand for quiet, intimate times with loved ones. She teaches and imparts all these attributes to those who come to know and love her gentle ways.

Chrysocolla Speaks:

Those who befriend me see and know
The stillness of water, the quiet flow.

Mild and loving, gentle but strong,
I sing to you a tranquil song.

Calming and patient, still and at rest,
I teach you that peace and silence are blest.

CHRYSOPRASE - *This green chalcedony is a member of the quartz clan.*

Gemstone Lore: This stone is associated with eloquence, expression and communication. It is also considered a balancing stone, promoting stability. Chrysoprase is further thought of as a stone that promotes adaptability, alternatives, choices and higher consciousness. It symbolizes the Earth at springtime, for this lovely stone is the color of newly-budding leaves—the young, hopeful, green color of the Earth at her rebirth. Chrysoprase is the maiden of the mineral clan. She is ever youthful and full of promise. Everywhere she graces with her fair presence radiates her aura of hope, zest, bright promise and a dash of the carefree wildness of youth. She is protective of all young life and is a good ally to have during any new venture or enterprise, for new beginnings are this stone's special love. She grants the hope of rebirth to all and imparts new mindsets to those who hold her near.

Chrysoprase is the patron stone of children, young animals and seedlings.

Chrysoprase Speaks:

I sing of the springtime, for out of the Earth
The soft buds of life bring the hope of rebirth.
I am the youth that still lives in your soul,
No matter how tired, no matter how old.

I bring the truth that spring comes anew
Ever from winter, that each soul can renew
Itself endlessly in lifetimes untold;
That the soul and the seasons alike unfold.

CITRINE - See page 60.

CORAL - *Coral is formed from the skeletons of tiny sea creatures.*

Gemstone Lore: WHITE CORAL has been traditionally linked with balance, relaxation, protection, safe travel on water and appreciation of nature. She is especially balancing of the emotions, having a soothing effect on her environment.

PINK CORAL is said to assist platonic love, friendship and community. Just as the tiny sea creatures band together to create a beautiful coral city in the sea, so Pink Coral teaches us to work together to build a beautiful reality here on earth.

RED CORAL is associated with creativity, passion, romantic love, wisdom, optimism and enthusiasm. Since romantic love and passion are often divorced from wisdom, it is good to keep Red Coral near at the beginning or "in love" stage of a relationship, for Red Coral can help us to stay centered and grounded in reality while still remaining enthusiastically passionate.

BLACK CORAL absorbs negative energy while increasing serenity and peace.

Lady Coral can attune us to the sea, and the sea's inhabitants. She has all the qualities of the ocean within her and knows the deep, calm mysteries of the sea as well as its vast, ancient power. And she will share all she holds within her depths, gently as the rising tide caressing the land with waves.

Spiritual Values of Gemstones

DIAMOND - *The hardest of all the gemstones, diamonds are clear and usually colorless.*

Gemstone Lore: Widely-held beliefs about the Diamond feature its ability in bonding relationships, protecting innocence and promoting hope. It encourages balance, clarity, profundity, discernment, love, abundance and courage.

This beautiful stone helps us get to the essence of things without being blinded by superficiality, for the Diamond knows full well how unimportant outer appearances are. Diamonds teach us to see through a person's outer package, into their depths. To see beneath the surface into the heart and soul—that is the Diamond's wisdom and gift to us.

BLACK DIAMONDS grant us the courage to look within without illusion. BLUE DIAMONDS inspire us to take better care of our health and strengthen will power. PINK DIAMONDS foster creative expression. YELLOW DIAMONDS make us more thoughtful and considerate.

EMERALD - *This green stone is a member of the beryl clan.*

Gemstone Lore: Emeralds promote love, cleansing, clairvoyance and all types of seeing because they open up the psychic eye and help the physical eye as well. The Emerald is traditionally thought of as a stone which strengthens memory and encourages all forms of love— romantic, spiritual and passionate. It is also a truth-promoting stone, inspiring deep knowing from within.

The combination of wisdom and clear vision makes

the Emerald an important friend for those who need to see clearly, from the heart. For this is very much a stone that combines the finest qualities of intellect and emotion, uniting them both with a strong foundation in love. Emeralds teach us to love all life unconditionally and at the same time perceive reality clearly.

Lady Emerald shows us that there is a difference between loving and being "in love." The latter involves seeing nothing but our own projections and illusions. The former involves seeing clearly and loving anyway. Emeralds show us that all living beings are lovable, if we look beyond the superficial, and that life on earth is worth living to the extent that we choose to be loving. For love is our choice. And this great wisdom is the Emerald's gift to us.

FLINT - *Flint is a gray, black or brown member of the quartz clan.*

Gemstone Lore: Tradition tells us that Flint augments loyalty, courage and protection. It is a stone of great spirit, fostering boldness, daring and self-reliance. Flint builds strength and power, teaching us to use these attributes to help the weak and oppressed. This stone teaches us to develop inner power as well and to use it wisely and for the good.

Flint is also regarded as a stone that fosters interpersonal communication by helping us to be more expressive of our real selves and feelings. It is therefore very useful for overcoming shyness.

Flint also inspired our early ancestors to make tools and build fires, not only to warm themselves but to keep away predatory animals. It is a stone of great inspiration and one which has been very protective of the human species, coming to our aid when times were hard. It does so to this day. When times are hard for us, then, Flint is ready and willing to inspire and protect us still.

Flint Speaks:

I was present at your species' birth
And taught you to survive on Earth
When human lives were hard and lean,
In an epoch called the Pleistocene.

Protecting you became my vow;
As I did then, I will do now!
For I have been here since time out of mind,
Warming and harboring humankind.

And you, in turn, shall serve the Light;
Protecting all nature, the truth and the right.

FLUORITE - *Fluorite is commonly white, yellow, blue, green or purple. Sometimes it is a mixture of any of these colors.*
Gemstone Lore: Fluorite is usually presented in the teachings as a psychic shield, unblocking energy while also energizing and protecting. This stone fosters truth, intellect and consciousness.

BLUE FLUORITE calms the emotions. PURPLE FLUORITE increases spiritual balance and mystic visions. YELLOW FLUORITE nurtures wisdom, knowledge and intelligence. WHITE FLUORITE builds purity of spirit.

A very protective stone, especially in the psychic

realm, Fluorite affords us safe journey to the world of spirit and is most helpful to persons attempting astral travel. Fluorite keeps us well balanced, with a foot in each world, even in the most transcendent of meditative states. This lovely stone opens us to the realization that there is a spirit world to be discovered and explored and then protects us when we journey to those numinous places.

Fluorite Speaks:

The spirit must journey to far lands and near,
To visit new worlds without worry or fear.

While your body remains at the place of your birth,
The spirit can travel beyond the green Earth.

To the stars and beyond, your soul must soar
As I stand loving watch at the spirit door.

GARNET - *This stone comes in a variety of colors, the most popular being red or green.*

Gemstone Lore: Down through the ages, RED GARNET has been linked to romantic love and passion, augmenting the sensual and even sexual within us. Lady Garnet knows the deep mysteries of intimacy and is therefore prized by lovers and those who wish to attract a lover. She also grants us positive thoughts and inspiration as part of her general energizing affect. This stone promotes the summoning up of ancient memories and therefore aids us in recovering memories of past life incarnations. Red Garnet is also associated with career success, social popularity and self-confidence.

Spiritual Values of Gemstones

GREEN GARNET fosters peace, serenity, meditation and creativity. It is especially useful during active meditative practices that combine centeredness and grounding with movement, such as Sufi dancing, yoga, Earth Religion Circles, Tai Chi or Aikido.

When Lady Garnet dons her green gown, she imparts a respect for all life and a healing, soothing presence combined with her active, inspirational soul. Thus she becomes the essence of spirituality in action, encouraging us to make our spiritual beliefs manifest in the world of action.

In her green form she is also associated with purification and patience—yet hers is the patience of those who wait not in passive surrender but with a peaceful, direct purpose.

Lady Garnet Speaks:

Adorned in red, I am love's delight—
The warmth of the fire, the passion of night.
I help to invoke, entice and inspire
Joyous expression of love and desire.

Bathed all in green I shine forth anew
To regenerate life, to refresh and renew.
Healing of soul and cleansing of heart,
Love is my power, patience my art.

GOLD - *A lustrous yellow when refined, gold is one of the elemental metals.*

Gemstone Lore: Traditional wisdom associates Gold with happiness, honor, generosity, strength of will and wealth. Gold is the metal sacred to the Sun God and, as such, embodies the God's attributes. Therefore, this metal inspires virtue, moral excellence and nobility of mind. He is a magnanimous metal, willing to share his strength and life-giving warmth with all. He stimulates the mental processes and promotes high-mindedness as well as positive thoughts. Gold augments good humor and high spirits, lending a cheering influence on his environment. He represents the best of masculine energy, enhancing courage and stimulating action.

Gold exerts a stabilizing influence on the character, strengthening and ennobling it. This life-loving metal teaches us that giving is sacred and that there is more than enough for all if we but share our bounty with others. Gold is considered a lucky metal of good fortune and opportunity. He is the patron metal of those who are generous, of all who give back to life.

GYPSUM - *Gypsum is a sedimentary rock, usually clear or white.*

Gemstone Lore: Gypsum is associated with prosperity, good luck and manifestation. It encourages us to make our dreams reality and create a positive environment for ourselves. Gypsum is considered lucky because it inspires us to bring our efforts to fruition, teaching us to reap our full rewards for a job well done. This is a stone that builds resolve and purpose, encouraging hard-working, honest, steady effort. Therefore it is good for those who would like to become more work-oriented and also for those who seek a satisfying, rewarding career.

Gypsum is a stone that is firm and fixed of purpose,

teaching us to stick to a job, a conviction or a person through thick and through thin. He is a stone of strong character and strength of will, imparting these attributes to all who befriend him. Gypsum is a dream weaver, or dream builder, guiding us firmly to expend the effort and take the steps to make our dreams come true. Keep him near when a project or venture becomes difficult or when all around you tell you your wishes cannot become reality. For Gypsum is an industrious dreamer, and he will add new hope and firm conviction to all your aspirations and plans.

Gypsum Speaks;

Steady of purpose, firm of hand,
Mine is the strength to hold to a plan,
To build the dream through good times and bad,
To enjoy the work with hearts made glad.

HAWK'S EYE - *This is a bluish-green to bluish-gray member of the quartz clan.*

Gemstone Lore: Hawk's Eye is associated with serenity, peace and perspective. Just as the hawk sees equally well at night and in the day, so the Hawk's Eye quartz teaches us to see both the dark and the light aspects of the earth plane. With him nearby, we can learn to come to terms with the imperfections of this world in a calm and discerning way. It is he who teaches us how to learn from all our experiences, to appreciate the workings of Karma and to seek a broader understanding of how all things ultimately work together for the good.

Crystal Wisdom

Hawk's Eye fosters abundance, prosperity and riches right here on the earth plane. For he teaches us that true abundance on Earth is found in an awareness and oneness with nature. It is realizing that you are bathed in gold every time you walk in the golden sunlight, that you are surrounded by jewels of emerald green whenever you go into a woodland dell, that there are no greater riches than the rich dark feel and touch of the abundant Earth beneath your feet. Hawk's Eye teaches you all this and awakens your life to prosperity beyond your wildest dreams. For to live as one with our sacred Earth Mother is to be bathed in good fortune always. Lord Hawk's Eye will gently lead you back to Her. Keep him near and you will find yourself getting outdoors more and appreciating it more. Then life on Earth will become rich, rewarding and satisfying.

Hawk's Eye Speaks:

I come to you in thankful prayer,
For endless riches are everywhere.

Open your heart, open your eyes
And your spirit will soar as the noble hawk flies.

Loving nature, touch the Earth—
And find the value of all life's worth.

HEMATITE - *Hematite is a reddish, gray or black iron ore.*

Gemstone Lore: Hematite is generally said to promote balance, focus, convergence and concentration of energy. He is a stone that helps us get to the heart or essence of things. Hematite is the scholar of the mineral clan, who teaches us to extract the substance from the appearance so that we can quickly learn that which we need to know. As he encourages the mind to focus and as he influences convergence on many levels, he also promotes the gathering together of people. So his is the gift to centralize ideas, energy and humans. Hematite is an excellent friend to place in the middle of a group to help it achieve like minds—among friends or in the family, too.

Hematite also builds reliability, confidence and trust. His is a steadying and a stabilizing presence. This stone has been traditionally considered to have a beneficial influence on legal situations because these situations often require sharp attention and the ability to distinguish between appearance and substance through meticulous analysis.

JADE - *Jade is usually green but can also come in a variety of colors.*

Gemstone Lore: Jade has been traditionally linked with serenity, wisdom, longevity, practicality and tranquility. Oriental cultures have long prized the Jade as a stone that can help unite the spiritual realm with the mundane world. It is seen as a stone of balance, peace and great knowing.

Jade is the sage, or wise old man of the gemstone world. His serenity is based on deep wisdom, for he knows how to live in harmony with the laws of nature and the laws of spirit. He can teach all who befriend him to live a life of moderation, always balancing the yin and the yang; giving equal consideration to the body, the mind and the spirit. He also teaches us to live in resonance with Mother Nature and celestial spirit equally. He passes on all that a wise old grandfather knows, helping us to gain perspective, equilibrium and stability.

BLACK JADE offers protection from negativity and the wise use of power. BLUE JADE inspires meditation. BUTTERFAT JADE brings relaxation. LAVENDER JADE inspires love, optimism and beauty. NEVADA JADE, also known as Nevada Lapis, brings healing ability and forgiveness, helping us become more agreeable, appreciative and life-affirming. ORANGE JADE enhances energy and protection. WHITE JADE fosters practical application of spirituality. YELLOW JADE is linked with assimilation, digestion, understanding and empathy.

JASPER - *This stone is usually red, yellow or brown and is a member of the quartz clan.*

Gemstone lore: Throughout the ages Jasper has been regarded as the stone of relaxation and contentment. This soothing and compassionate stone promotes mothering, nurturing and caring. Jasper is very supportive, lending deep tranquility to all who keep her near; for hers is a consoling and comforting presence.

Jasper represents the sun at its setting, the close of yet another day, the gentle turning of the universal rhythms. This mellow stone therefore signifies completion, wholeness and gentle endings. She teaches us that all things must end so as to make way for the new. Jasper shows us, for example, how to end relationships in a gentle, caring and kind way. She also offers perspective and solace to those who are grieving over the death of a loved one or the end of a relationship. Jasper is a good influence on people who have a hard time finishing tasks. This stone helps us to follow through, encouraging us to keep the enthusiasm alive until the task is done. This is a stone attuned to universal order and, as such, is good for those who have disorganized and scattered thoughts or who need more organizational ability. Jasper is the patron stone of counselors and therapists.

JET - *Jet is a form of coal. Its color is black.*

Gemstone Lore: Jet is associated with protection, optimism and emotional balance. He is the knight-errant of the mineral clan, protecting the defenseless and the weak and exerting his energies for justice and goodness. He is a gemstone of great nobility, honor and decency, teaching all who keep him near to fight for those who need help. Jet teaches us to be pure of heart, courteous and considerate; and he also shields us from negative thoughts and vibrations—our own and others'. This protective stone encourages us to stand our ground in the face of adversity. Jet is an optimistic gemstone, emanating cheer and happiness into the environment. He is filled with positive thoughts and feelings and doesn't know the meaning of the word surrender. Therefore, he helps us develop our own sense of purpose and confidence, especially when we face obstacles or opposition. Jet is also helpful during times of transition, as he facilitates acceptance of change and encourages growth, inner development and self improvement. Jet builds courage and leadership abilities as well, and is therefore helpful to those who are timid about translating their spiritual convictions into actions in the public arenas of life.

Jet Speaks:

I teach you honor and gallantry,
Guardianship and honesty,
And that even a humble piece of coal
Can transform itself to a higher goal.

In the face of change, be brave and bold,
Allowing the gem within to unfold.

KUNZITE - *Kunzite is a type of pink spodumene.*
Gemstone Lore: Kunzite promotes emotional balance, inner love, gentleness, friendliness and self-discipline. Those who befriend this stone are helped to attract gentle friends and are taught to combine compassionate self-love with discipline. It is therefore considered to be helpful in habit-breaking and in developing any type of self-discipline. Kunzite opens our sensitive selves and yet leads us to understand that kindness can also be strong. It teaches us that to love others we must love ourselves as well; it shows us how to unite strength and power with compassion and gentleness.

LABRADORITE - *Labradorite is a blue feldspar.*

Gemstone Lore: Labradorite not only strengthens our aura and assists us in developing our psychic powers, it also teaches us to use these powers wisely and well. A seeker of mysteries and an explorer of the occult, Labradorite is especially adept at helping us gain understanding of our own esoteric abilities. He shows us how to be comfortable in the presence of secret knowledge and power and so instructs us in using that power confidently and correctly.

A stone of strong will, he also helps build resolve and purpose. Labradorite aids us in communicating with our own highest power and with the Creator. He teaches us that we have many remarkable abilities we can tap and develop, and he encourages us to use these powers in a positive, life-loving way.

Keeping this wizard stone near reminds us that the path toward spiritual maturity and power requires dedication and perseverance. Just as the wizards of old served long apprenticeships and gradually gained their familiarity with the spirit powers, so too must we have the resolve to continue learning and exploring our own inner way.

LAPIS LAZULI - *The color is dark blue with gold flecks.*
Gemstone Lore: Throughout the ages, Lapis Lazuli has been regarded as the stone of truthfulness and as a strengthener of both mind and body. It makes us more open in all ways, including openness to psychic experience. This stone allows us to tap our own inner power and purifies the soul and the thoughts. Lapis Lazuli is also associated with self-confidence, tranquility and positive magic.

The dark blue Lapis bespeaks the power and mystery of the night sky. The golden specks within the deep blue are expressions of starlight. Lapis, the star goddess of the stones, knows the deep mysteries of night and space. It is she who understands the magic of the stars and brings a sense of power and wonder to all who befriend her. She opens the soul to spirit quests of the highest nature, teaching us to reach deep within our own great powers.

Lapis Speaks:

Pray with me, hold me close, under the stars.
All mystery, magic and wonder are ours.

I open your star powers from deep within.
I give you the strength to renew, to begin.

What better magic, O woman, O man,
Than to hold the night sky in the palm of your
*   hand!*

MALACHITE - *Malachite comes in varying shades of green.*

Gemstone Lore: This stone is associated with loyalty, healing dreams, emotional maturity, leadership ability and protection and is also thought to promote comfort, balance, peace and sensitivity. Malachite can help attune us to the spirit realm while keeping us grounded in the mundane world. It expands inner clarity and self understanding while encouraging transformation and healing. This growth-oriented stone is said to reflect the feelings of those who keep it near and to increase wisdom and the wise use of power. Malachite is also dedicated to purification and is thought to draw out negativity. Some people shy away from Malachite because of this cleansing aspect, which they feel can be temporarily upsetting. For whenever our old patterns of thought and behavior must make way for newer and better ways, the comfort of old habits are shaken; and our own inner world appears turbulent for awhile. Yet we must always be willing to die to the old to make a place for the new if we want to grow and evolve.

METEORITES - *Meteorites are shooting stars that land on Earth.*

Gemstone Lore: Meteorites are space travelers that have come to Earth. They have traveled long and far to bring us their cosmic wisdom. These space stones are considered excellent for channeling or communicating with celestial beings, the angelic realm, all extra-terrestrials and space travelers. They help us communicate directly with the Star Parents who seeded us here on earth, who are known to earthlings as all the many gods and goddesses. Our space parents still watch over us and protect us, and you can amplify prayers to them through a Meteorite. You can also hold a Meteorite up to the stars, on a clear night, and ask that it be enfused with star powers. Then it will put forth cosmic energies of celestial love and protection. And it will also help your own star powers to unfold so that you may see with starlight vision, for this is a stone of untold psychic wisdom. A Meteorite aids in the evolution of human kind, accelerating our mental growth and abilities.

MOONSTONE - *The color is usually milky, often with a yellowish or bluish tint. It is a type of feldspar.*

Gemstone Lore: Moonstone is generally said to promote good fortune, nurturing, mothering, unselfishness, happiness, humanitarian love, hope and spiritual insight. It has been traditionally believed to ease childbirth and protect those who travel on water. It is also considered to reflect emotions and feelings.

Moonstone is the stone of the Moon Goddess. She imparts all that is feminine, mysterious and loving in a gentle, nurturing way. Lady Moonstone reflects our feelings back to us, so we can get in touch with our emotions in order to use wisely our innermost feelings. An expression of the moon, this stone offers the hope of new beginnings just as the new moon offers the same. And as the full moon pours out the energies of abundance and fullness overflowing as mother's milk, so does Lady Moonstone. At the dark of the moon, the ancient wisdom of a wise old woman is poured upon the Earth in a time to meditate, dream, turn inward, and accept the death of the old so as to make way for the new. Moonstone imparts all these energies to us. When working with Moonstone it is best to attune her subtle yet powerful energies to the moon's phases. Then her power will come to the fore.

Moonstone Speaks:

I dance between the Sun and the Earth,
Granting you love, and the hope of rebirth.
From the heart comes truth, children of Earth,
Fear not your feelings, be assured of their worth.

Your feelings are kin to the tides of the sea.
Gently express them, and let them flow free.
The tides, like your feelings, ebb and they flow.
Unite them with spirit, so that you may grow.

Spiritual Values of Gemstones

MOSS AGATE - *Moss Agate is a greenish-brown member of the quartz clan.*

Gemstone Lore: Moss Agates increase prosperity, success and abundance. This stone also nurtures congeniality and compatibility and is therefore helpful when starting new friendships, when seeking a compatible lover or when trying to work on an old relationship that has gone awry.

Moss Agate is associated with healing, harmony and rain; it has a restorative effect on all living beings. This unifying stone links us to the plant kingdom, Devas or Nature Spirits. Our lives are made richer when we can communicate directly with the Nature Spirits, for they have an ancient wisdom and a healing love that we can tap. Moss Agate helps us bridge the communication gap between the human and plant clans so that we can speak to the flowers, the grasses, the herbs and the trees and in return understand all that they say. Moss Agate also aids fertility of plants. Placed in a plant pot or garden, it will help stimulate the growth of the green beings.

This harmonious stone fosters cooperation between people and nature, teaching us that for a whole and happy life, we must co-exist in concord and unity with all who share this beautiful planet with us.

Moss Agate Speaks:

Each blade of grass, each tiny flower
Is filled with healing wisdom and power.

Earth Mother calls to you, if you but heed
The trees of the forest, the buds of the mead.

Crystal Wisdom

The creatures of Nature grant knowledge untold,
And give back your love a thousandfold.

ONYX - *A member of the quartz clan, Onyx is usually*
black or brown with white bands.

Gemstone Lore: Increased vigor, strength and stamina are gifts of the Onyx. This stone can also enable us to become more stable, grounded, and settled. Infusing all who befriend it with constancy and steadfastness, it can assist us in "weathering the storm" in any situation and helps us create permanence and constancy through life's ups and downs. This stone aids us in finding that which is lasting, durable and worth hanging onto, and then gives us the tenacity to hold onto it firmly. It is an especially good friend to have when we need to adhere to our high values in the difficult or confusing times of our lives.

OPAL - *A member of the quartz clan. Opal comes in a*
wide range of colors.

Gemstone Lore: Love, loyalty, peace, consciousness and faithfulness are gifts of the Opal. Lady Opal is considered an emotional stone, reflecting the mood of the wearer. She can help those who wear her to be fully conscious of their own feelings. At times she has been represented as an unlucky stone, but this is only because modern people often fear and distrust their emotional side. Opal teaches us to express our innermost feelings and is especially helpful for those who have become withdrawn or shy about expressing their emotions. This stone can charm and entice those who are frightened about their feelings into opening up and becoming more warm, more spontaneous and more emotionally responsive.

Lady Opal is the patron stone of actors and performers, enlivening all who come to appreciate this grand lady with her dramatic, expressive flair. She is a sentimental and passionate stone, who shows us that when emotions are repressed, they become twisted into spite and coldness. When they are not repressed, our emotions flow with tenderness and sympathy.

BLACK OPAL promotes cosmic awareness and oceanic consciousness. BOULDER OPAL fosters creativity and originality. FIRE OPAL inspires dynamic energy and intensity. SONOMA OPAL induces emotional stability. WHITE OPAL enhances competency and efficiency.

PEARL - *Not actually a gemstone, Pearls evolve layer by layer in the matrix of living sea creatures.*

Gemstone Lore: Traditionally, the Pearl is understood to bring about greater purity, honesty, innocence and integrity. A refined and wholesome energy, the Pearl can help us get in tune with life's basic truths. It can align us with the simple honest things of life.

The Pearl helps us concentrate and focus our energy and is therefore very useful in meditation. This is a peaceful and serene energy, imparting tranquility to all who befriend it.

PERIDOT - *Peridot is also known as olivine or chrysolite. Its color is green.*

Gemstone Lore: Peridot is traditionally said to inspire purification, growth, intuition, healing, renewal and rebirth. This regenerating stone is considered soothing to the nerves and is good for alleviating anger, jealousy and irritation. Stress reduction and relaxation are gifts of Peridot as well. He is a stone of great vigor, lending a healthy glow to all who keep him near.

Peridot is traditionally associated with recuperative ability, encouraging us to bounce back from physical, emotional and even spiritual traumas. This stone helps us to remain strong and resilient. His bouyant and spirited energy enfuses the environment with a hopeful, healthy radiance—encouraging the life force to flow ever refreshed and renewed. Peridot grants relief and repose to those who are nervous or overwrought, for he is a stone of great comfort.

Peridot is the patron stone of healers. And he is especially good for healing the healers. This attribute is especially important today when so many people who work to heal the Earth, themselves and others talk about suffering "burnout." Peridot's calming influence helps us avoid burnout by reminding us that we do not have to save the world by ourselves, that the hurts we suffer in the struggle for peace can mend and that all action must come from a calm center to be effective.

PETRIFIED WOOD - *Petrified Wood is the fossilized form of ancient trees; it usually occurs in combinations of grays, reds and browns.*

Gemstone Lore: Petrified Wood enhances security, calmness, stability and strength. He bestows the gift of distant memories both ancient and wise and fosters longevity, wisdom and a respect for the aged. He leads us to respect tradition and seek out the knowledge of lost civilizations. He calls us back to all that is best and wise of the ancient ways.

Petrified Wood helps us to communicate with trees. The Tree Spirits stand ready to befriend us, to help us, to heal us—if we but stop and listen. We have much to gain by relating to trees, for they have an ancient knowledge that is different from and in many ways deeper than our own. Trees are the only beings on earth that reach the highest into the sky, tapping celestial, heavenly energy and simultaneously reach the deepest into the Earth to know the deep mysteries of our Earth Mother. Therefore trees have the most balanced energy of any being on Earth. And trees share this balancing influence, out of love, with anyone who befriends them.

PYRITE - *Pyrite is a member of the metallic mineral clan. Its color is yellow.*

Gemstone Lore: Pyrite is traditionally considered to be intellectually stimulating. He is the genius of the mineral clan and is thought to increase mental abilities, augment the intellect and stabilize the mind. Pyrite links the left hemishpere of the brain with the right and so facilitates communication between logic and emotions, analysis and creativity. This interconnection and flow between the two brain hemispheres promote a mental environment conducive to the unfolding of our talents, abilities, skills and gifts and the discovery of our individual genius. Each of us is, after all, a genius at something. For one person it might be mechanical ability, for another it might be understanding others' feelings. Pyrite unleashes our particular gift and allows it to flow.

Pyrite stimulates our highest mental abilities, promoting psychic development, memory, channeling abilities, optimism and strength of will. He teaches us to learn from both history and from our own past experience as this is the way to great wisdom, positive growth and change for the better.

Pyrite represents the sun at midday. He shines forth, illuminating everything with a clear, brilliant light. And this is the effect Pyrite has upon the mental processes. With dazzling focus and impressive discernment he brings insight, sagacity, perception and vision to all mental pursuits and is therefore a helpful companion in study, writing, or any analytical or intellectual effort.

Pyrite Speaks:

You hold in your hand a tiny sun
Uniting the heart and mind as one.

For I am the light of your highest mind,
Raising the powers of humankind

So that you may unfold and fulfill
Your own unique gift, your own special skill.

RHODOCHROSITE - *This is a peach-colored stone often banded with white.*

Gemstone Lore: This stone is dedicated to smooth energy flow. Generally healing to the emotions and the physical body, Rhodochrosite is considered to offer comfort, harmony, amity and friendship to those who keep it near.

Integrating various parts of our personality to form a

more harmonious blend is this stone's great gift. Rhodo-chrosite also promotes amity among people, but mainly it teaches us to befriend all the various parts of ourselves. This stone encourages us to integrate our previously disowned and ignored qualities into the greater whole, so that we can grow and evolve into more complete people. It augments tolerance, emotional awareness and self-love. Rhodochrosite also helps us develop kindness and compassion and to manifest these qualities in everyday life. In other words, it helps us live our spirituality.

ROSE QUARTZ - See page 91.

RUBY - *This red stone belongs to the corundum clan.*
　　Gemstone Lore: The Ruby is commonly accepted as the stone of happiness, healing, devotion and courage. This passionate stone can also facilitate romance, enthusiasm and excitement. It is an energizer and is therefore considered generally stimulating. This stone also fosters generosity, prosperity and leadership ability.
　　The Ruby evokes warmth and inspiration for all who hold it near. This ardent stone lends fire and power to all situations. The Ruby's ability to attract and enhance romantic love is heightened during the full moon.

SAPPHIRE - *Sapphires belong to the corundum clan and range in color from white to gray, blue and black.*
　　Gemstone Lore: Sapphires increase hope, faith, intelligence, wisdom, prophecy and happines.
　　The Sapphire helps its wearers get in touch with the realm of spirit, allowing their faith to become stronger.

This stone assures all that we are here for a purpose and that we are loved and protected by our Creator.

The Sapphire helps build our reliance and trust in goodness prevailing, and teaches increased faith in each other. This stone also encourages us to be more devoted, conscientious and trustworthy ourselves. Furthermore, the Star Sapphire is excellent for communicating with celestial beings such as angels and extraterrestrials.

DARK BLUE SAPPHIRE inspires creative expression, intuition and meditation. GREEN SAPPHIRE brings luck. ORANGE SAPPHIRE, also known as Padparadschah, augments wisdom, optimism and friendliness. PINK SAPPHIRE encourages generosity, love and loyalty. STAR SAPPHIRE develops independence, centering, balance and psychic powers. WHITE SAPPHIRE is associated with self-appreciation and spiritual development. YELLOW SAPPHIRE enhances intellect, study, knowledge and memory.

SARD - *A reddish-brown chalcedony, Sard is a member of the quartz clan.*

Gemstone Lore: Tradition has it that Sard builds independence, achievement and courage; for this stone is dedicated to liberation and self-determination. Sard also encourages us to trust our inner authority rather than continually seek elsewhere for guidance and insight. This is, moreover, a guardian stone especially protective of freedom, spontaneity and creativity.

For those who need to be more action-oriented and goal-directed, Sard is a good stone to befriend and keep near. He helps ground and center energy and can help make those who lack ambition more work-oriented. This is a stone of accomplishment, promoting completion of tasks and fulfillment of duties. A bold and daring ally of career and material success, Sard is the patron stone of entrepreneurial and business ventures. He is linked with achievement, success and victory. Sard also encourages us to find our life's work. This will be a vocation that brings us satisfaction as well as material rewards, while helping and healing ourselves and others.

SARDONYX - *This quartz clan member is a form of onyx with white and red bands.*

Gemstone Lore: According to conventional understanding, Sardonyx favors luck, friendship and happiness. This stone of good fortune is also considered helpful and healing to relationships and is therefore prized as an ally in romance and marriage.

Sardonyx watches over those who are young or a little wild, offering luck to those who take chances. This stone is the adventurer of the mineral clan. Sardonyx loves newness, challenge and exploration; he feels protective of all those who dare new things. His is a fearless energy and a strong one, too. This stone fosters stamina, vigor and boundless energy. Sardonyx also augments creativity and uniqueness. He brings his luck to those who are artists, writers and performers—those who try to make a living at creative expression.

Sardonyx is attuned to the wild beings of nature, for his is a free and untamed energy. When you go to a natural place, you might leave a Sardonyx there to help protect the wild Nature Spirits who dwell there. Those who feel overly timid, beaten down or afraid can meditate while holding a Sardonyx, allowing his dauntless energy to enliven their spirit. Sardonyx also helps us to remember our previous incarnations. Place him on the forehead (third eye) during meditations to get in touch with past lives.

SELENITE - *Selenite is a clear, crystalline gypsum.*

Gemstone Lore: It is traditionally said that Selenite is attuned to the highest plane. He is a stone of serenity, peace, meditation and universal consciousness. Selenite gets us in touch with our highest mind and promotes a feeling of oneness with the universe. He is much dedicated to clarity of thought and purity of heart. This is a stone of truth and universal love, encouraging his human friends to quest always towards the Creator, towards the good.

Selenite offers spiritual guidance and promotes psychic powers, especially mental telepathy. He can attune a group to develop a group mind and is therefore a stone of great worth when it comes to family harmony. Selenite is the patron stone of those who seek or hunger for spiritual attainment. This stone also fosters positive thoughts and clear thinking. Selenite helps us forgive; for he knows that if we harbor resentment or bitterness in our hearts, we cannot think clearly or positively.

Selenite Speaks:

The human heart is born to quest,
Always seeking the highest and best.

146

Spiritual Values of Gemstones

In deep meditation, in quiet prayer,
You'll find that perfection has always been there

From the beginning 'til time is done:
For you and the highest Creator are one.

SILVER - *Refined silver shines grayish-white. It is an elemental metal.*

Gemstone Lore: Traditional wisdom associates Silver with hope, meditation and unconditional, universal love. This lovely metal is sacred to the Moon Goddess and reflects the Goddess's attributes. Therefore, Silver fosters mothering nurturance, sympathy and gentle strength. She is a metal that grounds us on the earth plane, helping us to appreciate women and nature. Hers is a reflective, sensitive soul, promoting mystic dreams and visions. She teaches us to see with the moonlight vision—peering deep into the night, the soul, the subconscious—bringing to clarity all that is hidden and mysterious. This is a metal of the highest love and of romantic love as well, advancing romance while encouraging tenderness and kindness. Silver is a sensitive, feminine metal, purifying of heart and uplifting of spirit.

She is a metal of great psychic abilities and powers, fostering clairvoyance, telepathy, divination and astral travel. Silver is the patron metal of those who love and respect women, nature and the female principle of creation.

Silver Speaks:

You hold in your hands a tiny moonbeam
Aglow with a love that is soft as a dream—
Reflecting in shimmering, dancing moonlight
The metal most dear to the Lady of Night.
For mystery, kindness and love I esteem,
And all of wild nature I hold supreme.
The Feminine Spirit, both gentle and true,
And all of Her powers I grant unto you!

SMOKY QUARTZ - See Page 94.

SODALITE - *Sodalite's color is deep blue with white streaks.*

Gemstone lore emphasizes Sodalite's power to enhance rational thinking, logic, intelligence, emotional balance and higher knowledge. He therefore influences clear thinking, comprehension, depth of thought and perception. Sodalite is the deep thinker of the mineral clan. He facilitates knowledge, learning, proficiency, intuition, truth and consciousness.

Sodalite is the patron stone of those who seek wisdom. For he knows full well that attaining knowledge is not the same as attaining wisdom. Yet he is attuned to all learning and studying as one way ultimately to achieve deep discernment.

Sodalite is eager to teach humans that science, logic and rational thought, although important, are dangerous without loving spiritual wisdom to guide them. He is a stone that will help humans unite the logical with the spiritual—on both the individual and the cultural levels—thus bringing the left brain and the right into harmonious cooperation.

SUGILITE - *Sugilite, also known as luvulite, is dark purple.*

Gemstone Lore: Sugilite is seen as a stone which both enhances conscious awareness and also helps us relinquish negative thoughts and emotions.

Sugilite assists those who are very empathic and sensitve in coming to terms with the more difficult facts of corporeal existence and aids them in embracing life as it is. This stone can help the idealist, visionary and the extremely kindhearted soul retain their true vision and remain unhurt by the shocks and disappointments of the world. Sugilite is the practical saint of the mineral world—not a saint who suffers but one who combines a peaceful and joyful life of the soul with true help and kindness for all living things.

Sugilite Speaks:

I can walk amidst squalor, aid the hurt and the lame,
Yet my spirit shines strong as a glowing bright flame.
I feel all beings' hunger, sadness and fears,
Yet I sing as I feed them and wipe away tears.

Crystal Wisdom

The ecstatic joy of life I can feel too;
The empath must tap that to heal and renew.
Close not your heart to another's pain
But stay open to sunshine, as well as to rain.

The Creator gave you a sensitive soul
To make the universe better and whole.

TIGER'S EYE - *This member of the quartz clan is a rich brown color with shimmers of gold running through it.*

Gemstone Lore: Tiger's Eye enhances protection, clear thinking, personal empowerment, integrity, will-power, practicality and the integration of spirit with mundane energy. Its form and colors call to mind the fertile Earth warmed by the sun.

This is a stone of great power, enabling all who draw near its aura to tap their own inner power and then use it wisely. This is also a stone of great will that helps us strengthen our own willpower. This stone teaches us to see with the eye of the tiger: clearly and without illusion. It grants the wearer courage, will, strength and grace.

The Tiger's Eye, in addition, integrates the heat, passion and glaring truth of the sun with the receptive, dark, cool fertility of the Earth. From this unification within ourselves comes both inner power and the ability to nurture and create with that power. The integration and balance of male and female energy is also facilitated by Tiger's Eye. From this balance, we can more fully develop our strength along with gentleness.

RED TIGER'S EYE teaches us to be energetic in a very composed, serene way.

Spiritual Values of Gemstones

Tiger's Eye Speaks:

*Bright warmth of Sun Father, dark womb of the
   Earth,
Uniting in love to give all life its birth,
I bring you hope to renew and begin,
Tapping deep power and strength from within.*

*Man and woman, Earth and Sun,
Join in love to become as one.*

TOPAZ - *Topaz is usually a golden yellow but can also be
   brown or pink.*

Gemstone Lore: Topaz increases good fortune, happiness and hope. This stone is also seen as a teacher of spiritual love which tends to induce a feeling of peace in those who come to appreciate it.

Topaz emanates benevolence and joy to all who befriend it. This stone suffuses its surroundings with vibrations of contentedness, cheerfulness and gaiety.

Topaz also attracts love and synchronicity into one's life.

BLUE TOPAZ inspires leadership ability, psychic knowing, spiritual growth, tranquility and psychic insight. CLEAR TOPAZ helps us communicate with Devas (Nature Spirits) and with all the animals and plants of the Earth. GOLDEN TOPAZ builds generosity, humor, optimism, creativity, wisdom, inspiration, abundance and love. GREEN TOPAZ guides us towards forgiveness and understanding. PINK TOPAZ promotes honor and truth.

TOURMALINE - *Tourmaline's color range is immense. It can range from clear white all the way to black.*

Gemstone Lore: Tourmaline's attributes include the power to enhance flexibility, happiness, objectivity, compassion, serenity, balance, positive transformation, healing and strength. This is a stone that allows us to be flexible and tolerant. It is a stone that reminds us that we are connected to all life and all range of expression. It helps us achieve better understanding of complexity, and it enables us to flow with life.

Tourmaline is an excellent channel to the higher forces and is often used in conjunction with praying to celestial beings or communicating with extra-terrestrials.

Tourmaline teaches us that the light shines in many colors, many expressions and that as long as a person walks a positive spiritual path, we should accept their belief system as good for them. We should not judge others or be intolerant. Tourmaline teaches us that there are many paths to the light.

BLUE TOURMALINE is also known as Indicolite or Indigolit. It is linked with peace, balance, eloquence and emotional purification. COLORLESS TOURMALINE (Achroite) brings contact with the angelic realm. BLACK TOURMALINE protects us from negative energy. BROWN TOURMALINE encourages stability and practicality. GREEN TOURMALINE is said to foster prosperity, success, general healing, strength, purification and communication. YELLOW TOURMALINE brings heightened intelligence and spiritual awareness. VIOLET TOURMALINE inspires meditation. PINK TOURMALINE attunes us to love and opens the heart. MULTI-

COLORED TOURMALINE teaches us to live harmoni-
ously with the whole range of humanity.

Tourmaline Speaks:

Come with me, change with me, bend with the flow.
Upon many paths I have watched humans go.

Do not judge them wrong, but know they are right—
If there's kindness to life, then they walk in the Light.

To help your mind open, to live in the Tao,
To teach peace and tolerance, that is my vow.

TURQUOISE - *The colors in Turquoise range from blue to green.*
Gemstone Lore: Turquoise is usually linked with
protection, balance, strength, energy, wisdom, serenity and
friendship. This stone encourages positive thinking and is
considered to be generally healing.

Turquoise is an empathic stone. And just as it tends to
take on the attributes of those who wear it, it also teaches the
wearer to be more empathic, or sensitive to the feelings and
attributes of others around them. It can help make us more
sensitive to all life and help us learn that we are all one.

Because Turquoise symbolizes the desert sky at midday—clear blue and limitless--this stone helps us realize that
there are no boundaries between ourselves and others and no
limits to the spirit. Turquoise connects us to the All, gently
urging us to become one with all life and with the universe.

Crystal Wisdom

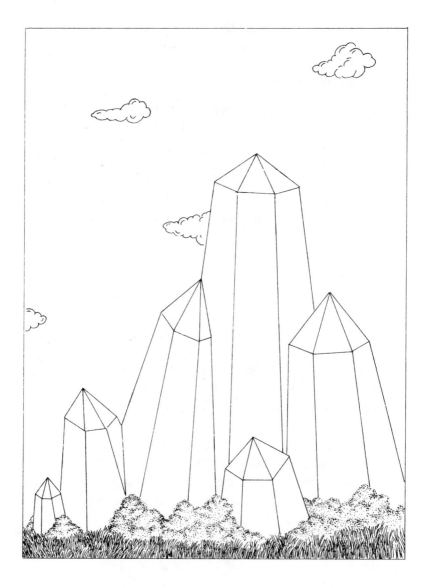

CHAPTER VI

A CONCISE LISTING OF LESS FAMILIAR STONES

ABALONE - Is associated with healing, serenity, calmness, nobility, and honesty.

ACTINOLITE - The color is green. This stone is associated with creative expression, appreciation of beauty and spontaneity. This is also an excellent stone for improving visualizations and mental imagery.

ALBITE FELDSPAR - White, gray, clear or bluish. Promotes stability, constancy, balance. Inspires us to become spiritual leaders by sharing our unique truths.

ALEXANDRITE - A green form of Chrysoberyl. Encourages regeneration, renewal, protection, joy, emotional maturity, purity, grace and elegance.

ALMANDINE - A red Garnet with a violet tint. Brings

spirituality to relationships. Helps in the transition from romance to a spiritual commitment in love.

AMBLYGONITE - Golden-yellow to clear. Develops empathy, self-confidence, thoughtfulness, self-esteem.

ANDALUSITE - Yellow, green or brownish-red. Promotes career success, ascendancy, authority, leadership ability, and wise use of power.

ANGLESITE - A white metallic mineral. Promotes sensitivity, gentleness, relaxation and tenderness.

ANORTHITE FELDSPAR - White, gray or glassy. Brings balance, wholeness, integration and stability.

ARAGONITE - A form of Calcite. White, cream or gray. Fosters truth, emotional stability and inner understanding.

ARIZONA AGATE - Is linked with sensuality, pleasure, emotional warmth, earthiness, happiness and prosperity.

AUGITE - Green to black. Is associated with prosperity, success, good fortune and luck.

AUTINITE - Green. Fosters courage, daring, new beginnings and adventures. Protective of the young and free.

AXINITE - Blue, violet or brown. Teaches us to activate and live our spirituality in our daily lives.

BARITE - Wide color range. Is linked with platonic love, friendship, loyalty, love, communication and intimacy.

BENITOITE - Light to dark blue. Is associated with emotional sensitivity, empathy and understanding.

BERYL - An ore of beryllium. CLEAR BERYL: Also called Goshenite. Intellectual abilitiy, wisdom, objectivity. **GOLDEN BERYL:** Also called Heliodor. Persistence, altruism, spirituality, healing, strength, learning, communication, comfort. **PINK BERYL:** Also called Morganite or Bixbite. Tolerance, empathy, love, acceptance.

BERYLLIUM - Is associated with altered states, meditation and cosmic consciousness.

BLUE QUARTZ - Inspires spiritual development, meditation, psychic abilities and serenity.

BORNITE - A metallic mineral with a purple tarnish. Fosters peace, social justice, goodness, fairness, truth, equality and caring on a worldwide scale.

BRAZILIANITE - Yellow or greenish-yellow. Academic ability, attention to detail, study skills, intelligence.

BRONZE - Is associated with relaxation, serenity, calmness. Helps promote a laid-back attitude.

CASSITERITE - A tin oxide, usually brown or black. Promotes productivity, practicality and organization.

CAT'S EYE - Also known as Cymophane. Builds determination, strength of mind, will power, moral courage, tenacity, vigor, intelligence, constancy and stability.

CERUSSITE - Clear, gray, brown. Inspires contentment and a feeling of thankfulness. Teaches us how to pray.

CHALCOPYRITE - A brassy-gold copper ore with a green tint. Enhances feelings of self-worth, confidence and belief in oneself.

CHLORITE - Usually green. A stone of the Goddess. Protective of women, nature, those who love the Earth.

CINNABAR - Also called Mercury. Usually red. Helps us to be vigorous, forceful, energetic and assertive.

CLINOZOISITE - Light green to brownish-green. Teaches us to care for ourselves and encourages us not to let others take advantage of us.

COBALT - Fosters channeling, communication with the higher forces, balance, praying and thankfulness.

COBALTITE - The color is silver. Associated with re-flection, meditation, re-evaluation, thoughtfulness, care-ful consideration and tolerance.

COLEMANITE - Translucent. Helps us become more yin: gentler, sweeter, quieter. Helps us mellow out.

COPPER - This metal promotes channeling, cleansing, luck, prosperity, purification, self-esteem, communica-tion and energy. It is often used as the shaft of crystal wands because it facilitates the flow of energy.

COVELLITE - A blue metallic mineral. Helps us focus our energy and expend it with direction and effectiveness.

CUPRITE - Red. Encourages pragmatism, focus, help-fulness and morality.

DANBURITE - Colorless, pink or yellow. Increases patience, tolerance, serenity, peace of mind.

DATOLITE - Greenish. Builds clarity of thought, con-centration, study skills, flow of ideas, mature thought.

DESAUTEKITE - Is associated with clairvoyance, psy-chic abilities and seeing the future. Helps us during divination, such as Tarot, I-Ching, palmistry and so forth.

A Concise Listing of Less Familiar Stones

DIABASE - Makes one more potent, forceful, powerful, effectual, capable, strong and energetic.

DIOPSIDE - A green member of the pyroxene clan. Helps us become more appreciative of life.

DIOPTASE - Green. Relieves mental stress and promotes prosperity, relaxation, meditation, love and emotional expressiveness. Is said to be generally healing.

DUMORTIERITE - Dark blue, violet blue or reddish brown. Promotes harmony, orderliness, precision, self-discipline and the ability to organize. Helps us become more businesslike, systematic, tidy and methodical.

EILAT - A Chrysocolla containing Turquoise and Malachite. Inspires protection, self-understanding, subconscious wisdom, general healing, harmony and sociability.

ENARGITE - Green, brownish-green, gray, yellow. Is associated with sages, medicine men and women, shamans, priests and priestesses. Helps us develop our wisest, highest self. Helps us find our inner guide.

ENSTATITE - Green, gray, yellow or brownish-green. Promotes loyalty, devotion, memory and channeling.

EPIDOTE - The color ranges from green to brown and black. Also called Pistacite. Epidote is associated with protection, empowerment, change, growth, maturity, evolution, positive transformation, and fulfillment.

EUCLASE - Colorless, green or light blue. Facilitates benevolence, selflessness, generosity and altruism.

FAIRY STONE - Brown to black in color. Also called Staurolite or Fairy Cross. Associated with luck, positive magic, happiness, love of life, enthusiasm, love of nature.

FUCHSITE - Green. Promotes diplomacy, discretion, imagination, creativity and appreciation of beauty.

GALENA - An important source of lead. Promotes healing, calmness, communication, efficiency, receptivity, sensitivity, competency, intelligence and insight.

GEODES - Foster intellectual insight, awareness and community. Geodes help us attract compatible friends and lovers and teach us to live in harmony with each other.

GOSHENITE - A clear Beryl. Promotes practical wisdom, moderation, intellectual curiosity and well-thought-out decisions. Helps those who have a hard time making decisions.

GRANITE - Encourages us to go with the flow, and find our highest path. Teaches us to live in a state of grace.

GROSSULARITE - A type of Garnet. Clear, brownish, yellow or green. This stone enhances energy, prosperity and career success. BROWN GROSSULARITE encourages balance and serenity. It also helps us acquire land or property. CLEAR GROSSULARITE is associated with spiritual attainment. GREEN GROSSULARITE promotes healing. YELLOW GROSSULARITE enhances calmness, enducing meditation and relaxation.

HALITE - Helps us transcend our problems. Encourages perspective and contentment.

HAMBERGITE - Colorless or white. Helps us stick to our beliefs. Fosters idealism, character and truth.

HAUYNITE - A transparent blue. Helps us gain respect,

honor, esteem and admiration.

HEMIMORPHITE - Also known as Calamine. Blue, green, clear. Fosters enthusiasm, optimism, high energy and the ability to stay with a project right to the end.

HIDDENITE - A yellow-green to green member of the Spodumene clan. Grants spiritual attainment, enlightenment, universal compassion, transcendence and peace.

HOWLITE - Snowy white, sometimes with brown or black veins. Rarely clear. Fosters appreciation of beauty, inspiration, creativity and artistic expression.

HYACINTH - See Zircon, page 168.

HYPERSTHENE - Blackish brown, blackish green. Enhances self-esteem, emotional expression and overcoming shyness. Helps put us at ease in all social situations.

ICELAND SPAR - See Calcite, page 114.

INDICOLITE - See Tourmaline, page 152.

IOLITE - Blue. Enhances leadership ability, power, inner strength, self-confidence and executive ability.

IRON - Promotes balance, strength, endurance, protection, longevity, persistence, emotional stability, favorable legal situations, efficiency and skill.

IVORY - Is best left on the elephant or walrus. Let us protect and respect these intelligent and sensitive animals.

JADEITE - Wide range of colors. Encourages emotional balance, a sense of well being and healing dreams.

KORNERUPINE - Green or greenish-brown. Enhances

teaching ability, eloquence, communication and clarity.

KYANITE - Clear, blue, blue-green. Also called Disthene. Augments channeling, altered states, vivid dreams, clear visualization, loyalty, honesty and serenity.

LACE AGATE - Quartz. BLUE LACE AGATE is associated with hope, unity, cleansing, harmony, protection, optimism, positive thinking, appreciation for nature, smooth energy flow, joy, truth, purification and promptness. Makes us more easygoing. MEXICAN LACE AGATE is said to lift depression. PINK LACE AGATE increases friendliness and happiness. WHITE LACE AGATE attunes us to our highest mind and to the Creator.

LAZULITE - Blue-white to dark blue. Inspires tranquillity, self-esteem. Is good for those who feel stressed out.

LEAD - See Galena, page 160.

LEPIDOLITE - Promotes spiritual transcendence, cosmic awareness, emotional balance, meditation, prayer and goodness. Is considered helpful for insomniacs.

LEUCITE - Colorless, white. Encourages reconciliation with friends and lovers. Facilitates tolerance and empathy.

LIMESTONE - Is said to enhance healing, purification, innocence, centeredness and positive thoughts.

LLANOITE - Encourages individuality, expressiveness, originality and creativity.

LODESTONE - See Magnetite, page 163.

LUDLAMITE - A relaxation stone fostering comfort, ease, rest, repose and mellowness. Good for workaholics.

LUVULITE - See Sugilite, page 149

MAGNETITE - A black iron ore. It is a magnetized stone. Magnetite promotes love, good luck, health, stability, strength, perspective, mental telepathy, visualizations and prayers.

MARBLE - Encourages gentleness, tenderness and love. Teaches us the art of listening.

MARCASITE - Also called White Pyrite. Marcasite inspires relaxation, reflection, spiritual development, focus and clarity. It encourages past life recall and awakens ancient memories.

MELANITE - A black type of andradite. Garnet clan. Opens our psychic vision for forecasting, divination and seeing the future. Brings an understanding and acceptance of death, rebirth and reincarnation.

MILLERITE - Promotes reason, moderation, tolerance, frugality and efficiency.

MOLDAVITE - A green meteorite. Especially good for channeling healing energy. Helps us to communicate with our higher self and with extra-terrestrials.

MOLYBDENITE - Soft, metallic and opaque with a blue-gray streak. Helps us tap subconscious knowledge, face our hidden self, and develop our character.

MUSCOVITE - A pale, almost clear mica. Facilitates astral projection, contact with angels and spirit guardians.

NATROLITE - White, yellowish. Is associated with achievement, success, victory and triumph. Helps us overcome challenges to reach our goals.

163

NEPHRITE - Wide color range. Brings inner strength, fortitude, courage, protection, persistence and completion. Helps us stand our ground.

OLIVINE - See Peridot, page 139.

ORPIMENT - Is associated with innocence, purity, goodness, nurturance and emotional intimacy. Helps us choose friends and lovers wisely.

ORTHOCLASE - A champagne-yellow feldspar. Helps overly intellectual become heart-centered and grounded.

PADPARADSCHAH - See Sapphire, page 143.

PETALITE - Colorless, pink. Is associated with inspiration, fertility and imagination.

PHENACITE - Colorless, pink or yellow. Helps those who have addictive personalities overcome their negative habits. Especially good for those who are addicted to love.

PHOSGENITE - Clear, yellow-white, greenish, white. Is associated with boldness, courage, daring and confidence.

PIEMONTITE EPIDOTE - Is associated with leadership, direction, energy, purposeful activity and liveliness.

PRASIOLITE - A leek-green member of the Quartz clan. Inspires self-reliance and originality. Gives us the courage to dare new things.

PREHNITE - Yellow-green, yellow-brown. Facilitates trustworthiness, truth, calmness, sincerity and sensitivity.

PURPURITE - Purple, pink or brown. Brings vitality, hardiness, vigor, stamina and rejuvenation.

PYROLUSITE - Is associated with hope, optimism, con-

A Concise Listing of Less Familiar Stones

fidence, determination and material comfort.

PYROPE - A red Garnet with a brown tint. Brings stability in relationships. Helps in the transition from romance to firm commitment in love.

REALGAR - The color is orange-red. Associated with introspection, insight, balance, meditation and harmony.

RHODONITE - Red with black inclusions. Brings calmness, self-confidence, gracefulness, elegance, courtesy, tact, alternatives and inner growth. Helps us reach our full potential. Teaches us to see both sides of the issue.

SCAPOLITE - Yellow, violet, pink or clear. Also called Wernerile. Facilitates integration of the mind and the heart. Helps the overly emotional person become more analytical.

SCHEELITE - Clear, yellow, brown, orange. Is associated with mental balance and well-being, clarity of thought and emotional moderation.

SERPENTINE - Various hues of green. Inspires respect for the elderly, longevity, retrieval of ancient wisdom and remembrance of past lives.

SINHALITE - A yellow or greenish-brown. Inspires change, growth, improvement, regeneration and the ability to see a task through to the end.

SMITHSONITE - Also known as Bonamite. BLUE SMITHSONITE fosters emotional expressiveness. GREEN SMITHSONITE is associated with renewal, rebirth and new beginnings. PINK SMITHSONITE helps us attract new friends. PURPLE SMITHSONITE awakens psychic abilities. YELLOW SMITHSONITE increases energy.

SPECTRALITE - Is associated with renewal, invigoration, energy, health and regeneration.

SPESSARTITE - An orange or red-brown Garnet. Helps us attract a home and put down roots. Promotes self-love.

SPHALERITE - Yellow, green, clear. Is said to enhance relaxation, rest, ease, gentleness and caring.

SPHENE - Yellow, brown, green. Also called Titanite. Offers comfort, consolation, encouragement and balance.

SPINEL - Comes in a variety of colors. Augments renewal, allowing us to refresh and restore ourselves time and time again. It is associated with hope, will and purpose, encouraging us to overcome all obstacles. BLACK SPINEL fosters protection. BLUE SPINEL soothes and calms, bringing peace and transcendence. GREEN SPINEL facilitates healing, communication and wisdom. ORANGE SPINEL inspires optimism. PURPLE SPINEL encourages us to serve the forces of goodness and light. It also fosters communication between the generations. RED SPINEL energizes and strengthens.

SPODUMENE - GREEN SPODUMENE enhances the ability of healers. PINK SPODUMENE (see Kunzite, page 132). YELLOW SPODUMENE promotes spirituality and connects us with our higher self.

STAR GARNET - Enhances career success, respect, fame, glory, empowerment, renown and increased productivity.

SULPHUR - Yellow. Helps wishes, thoughtforms, positive visualizations to become reality. Healing.

SUNSTONE - Also called Aventurine Feldspar or Oligoclase. An orange to red-brown feldspar. Inspires originality, romance, sexuality, independence and luck.

TANTALITE - A dark brown or black metallic ore. Tantalite promotes love, intensity, desire, passion and excitement. It builds energy, enthusiasm and a love of life.

TANZANITE - A blue form of Zoisite. Is linked with composure, poise and harmony. Teaches us to slow down and take it easy. Good for workaholics.

TEKTITE - Promotes extra-terrestrial communication and contact. Develops wisdom and knowledge.

THULITE - A red form of Zoisite. Teaches us to be passionate in a grounded, realistic way. Excellent for perspective during the "in love" phase of a relationship.

TOURMALINATED QUARTZ - Black Tourmaline crystals inside of clear crystals. Balances and unites conscious with subconscious, male with female, spirit with matter, heaven with earth. Brings harmony to any polarity and brings moderation and unity to all situations.

ULEXITE - White. Teaches us to see through the superficial into the soul within. Helps us gain inner depth and develop spiritual values.

VANADINITE - Fosters spiritual insight, prayer, meditation and direct communication with the higher forces.

VARISCITE - Green-yellow, blue. Augments moral courage, virtue, self-reliance and success. Is also considered emotionally calming and soothing. Helps us remember our past lives.

VEATCHITE - Helps us develop a sense of humor, lightness and fun. Inspires communication with nature.

VESUVIANITE - Olive green, brownish-yellow. Also called Idocrase. Passion, enthusiasm, warmth, devotion.

VIOLANE - Violet. Pyroxene clan. Helps us develop a feeling of gratitude, thankfulness and appreciation. Teaches us to count our blessings.

WILLEMITE - Yellow, reddish-brown, greenish. Is associated with caring and tenderness. Helps us to be kind and empathic to all beings.

WITHERITE - Clear, yellow, white. Helps us to be modest without being too humble.

WULFENITE - Orange, red, honey-colored yellow. Teaches us to be stewards and caretakers of all the wild and beautiful places of nature. Fosters creativity and devotion.

ZIRCON - Is also known as Hyacinth. BLUE ZIRCON fosters spirituality and praying. BROWN ZIRCON inspires independence. It also helps us attract land and a permanent home. GREEN ZIRCON promotes renewal and friendliness. PINK ZIRCON helps us appreciate life more. PURPLE ZIRCON enhances prosperity. RED ZIRCON is for purification. YELLOW ZIRCON brings inspiration.

ZOISITE - Enhances self-control, temperance, self-esteem, healing, harmony, dream recall, relaxation and responsibility. Good for insomniacs.

REFERENCE CHART

THE SPIRIT STONES

SPIRITUAL DEVELOPMENT - Amethyst, Beryl (golden), Citrine, Calcite (white) Celestite, Clear Quartz Crystals, Meteor Crystals, Rhodochrosite, Selenite, Seven-Faceted Crystals, Sugilite, Topaz, Window Crystals.

TRUTH, HONESTY - Amazonite, Celestite, Chrysocolla, Citrine, Emerald, Fluorite, Jet, Kyanite, Lapis Lazuli, Pearl, Ruby, Selenite, Seven-Faceted Crystals, Sodalite, Tiger's Eye.

MEDITATION - Amethyst, Aquamarine, Chrysocolla, Clear Quartz Crystals, Double Terminated Crystals, Garnet (green), Quantum Crystals, Sapphire (blue), Selenite, Tourmaline (violet), Turquoise.

HARMONY - Agate, Amethyst, Apatite, Carnelian, Clear Quartz Crystal, Coral (pink), Crystal Cluster, Jade, Rhodochrosite, Rhodonite, Selenite, Seven-Faceted Crystals, Tourmaline (multi-colored).

PEACE - Amethyst, Apatite, Aquamarine, Chrysocolla, Fluorite (blue), Garnet (green), Hawk's Eye, Jade, Malachite, Opal, Rose Quartz, Selenite, Sugilite, Topaz, Tourmaline (blue).

SERENITY - Aquamarine, Chrysocolla, Emerald, Garnet (green), Hawk's Eye, Jade, Jasper, Kunzite, Kyanite, Lapis Lazuli, Pearl, Selenite, Seven-Faceted Crystals, Smoky Quartz, Tourmaline, Turquoise.

PATIENCE - Amber, Azurite, Chrysocolla, Garnet (green), Left-Handed Crystals.

TOLERANCE - Agate, Chrysocolla, Receiving Crystals, Rhodochrosite, Rose Quartz, Tourmaline (multi-colored).

FORGIVENESS - Chrysoberyl, Nevada Jade, Selenite, Topaz (green).

THE HEART STONES

LOVE - Abundance Crystals, Agate, Amber, Apatite, Chrysocolla, Coral (pink), Topaz, Diamond, Dolphin Crystals, Emerald, Lapis Lazuli, Moonstone, Opal, Rose Quartz, Selenite, Soulmate Crystals, Tourmaline (pink), Turquoise.

KINDNESS, SENSITIVITY - Artemis Crystals, Azurite, Celestite, Chalcedony, Chrysoberyl, Chrysocolla, Empathic Crystals, Jasper, Kunzite, Rhodochrosite, Rose Quartz, Selene Crystals, Sugilite, Tourmaline, Turquoise.

ROMANCE, PASSION - Amber, Coral (red), Emerald, Garnet (red), Opal, Rose Quartz, Ruby, Sardonyx, Soulmate Crystals.

169

THE MIND STONES

WISDOM - Amber, Gold, Calcite, Chrysocolla, Clear Quartz Crystals, Coral (red), Dolphin Crystals, Emerald, Fluorite (yellow), Jade, Labradorite, Malachite, Merlin Crystals, Milky Quartz, Smoky Quartz, Sapphire, Sodalite, Moonstone, Pearl, Petrified Wood, Sapphire (orange), Turquoise.

IMAGINATION, CREATIVITY - Abundance Crystals, Agate, Aventurine, Carnelian, Citrine, Coral (red), Double Terminated Crystals, Garnet (green), Herkimer Diamonds, Left-Handed Crystals, Muse Crystals, Pyrite, Sapphire (blue).

INTELLECT - Apatite, Azurite, Beryl, Calcite (gold), Emerald, Fluorite (yellow), Hematite, Pyrite, Sapphire, Sodalite, Right-Handed Crystals.

MEMORY - Calcite (gold), Carnelian, Clear Quartz Crystal, Emerald, Pyrite.

THE WIZARD STONES

MANIFESTATION OF WISHES - Abundance Crystals, Artemis Crystals, Carnelian, Clear Quartz Crystals, Gypsum, Labradorite, Lapis Lazuli, Merlin Crystals, Obsidian, Quantum Crystals, Smoky Quartz, Wand Crystals.

TRANSFORMATION - Amethyst, Azurite, Clear Quartz Crystals, Jet, Malachite, Obsidian, Tourmaline.

THE ABUNDANCE STONES

PROSPERITY, ABUNDANCE - Abundance Crystals, Agate, Aventurine, Bloodstone, Chalcedony, Citrine, Diamond, Eight-Faceted Crystals, Garnet (red), Gypsum, Hawk's Eye, Moonstone, Ruby, Sard, Topaz.

GOOD LUCK - Abundance Crystals, Agate, Bloodstone, Gold, Moonstone, Gypsum, Sapphire (green), Sardonyx, Topaz.

GENEROSITY - Agate, Amber, Bloodstone, Chalcedony, Chrysoberyl, Citrine, Gold, Moonstone, Ruby.

THE GUARDIAN STONES

PROTECTION - Abundance Crystals, Agate, Alexandrite, Citrine, Coral (white and black), Crystal Clusters, Dolphin Crystals, Flint, Fluorite, Labradorite, Jet, Malachite, Sard, Sardonyx, Tiger's Eye, Turquoise, Wand Crystals.

INDEPENDENCE, FREEDOM - Artemis Crystals, Aventurine, Carnelian, Parity Crystals, Sard.

THE JOYOUS STONES

HAPPINESS, OPTIMISM - Carnelian, Chrysoberyl, Chryso-

170

prase, Coral (red), Jet, Moonstone, Onyx, Pyrite, Rainbow Crystals, Ruby, Sapphire, Smoky Quartz, Sardonyx, Topaz, Tourmaline.

HOPE - Chrysoberyl, Chrysocolla, Diamond, Moonstone, Rainbow Crystals, Sapphire, Topaz.

JOY - Alexandrite, Emerald, Lifepath Crystals, Smoky Quartz, Topaz, Sugilite.

SOCIABILITY, OVERCOMING SHYNESS - Carnelian, Chalcedony, Citrine, Crystal Clusters, Flint, Garnet (red), Kunzite, Moss Agate, Opal, Rhodochrosite, Sardonyx, Turquoise.

THE GROUNDING STONES

STABILITY, SECURITY - Chrysoprase, Citrine, Gypsum, Hematite, Jade, Kunzite, Obsidian, Onyx, Petrified Wood, Smoky Quartz.

APPRECIATION OF NATURE - Agate, Amethyst, Aquamarine, Artemis Crystals Carnelian, Coral, Devic Crystals, Enchanted Crystals, Hawk's Eye, Petrified Wood, Rainbow Crystals, Sardonyx, Silver, Topaz (clear).

PRACTICALITY - Gypsum, Jade, Obsidian (black), Pyrite, Sard, Smoky Quartz, Tiger's Eye, Worldly Crystals.

THE EMPOWERING STONES

SELF-ESTEEM, SELF-LOVE - Amazonite, Carnelian, Copper, Kunzite, Rhodochrosite, Rhodonite.

INNER POWER, WILLPOWER - Aquamarine, Eight-Faceted Crystals, Flint, Gypsum, Kunzite, Labradorite, Lapis Lazuli, Pyrite, Ruby, Rutilated Quartz, Tiger's Eye.

CONFIDENCE - Citrine, Garnet (red), Hematite, Jet, Lapis.

COURAGE - Agate, Carnelian, Diamond, Flint, Hematite, Herkimer Diamonds, Jet, Tiger's Eye, Ruby, Rutilated Quartz, Smoky Quartz, Sard, Sardonyx, Tiger's Eye.

THE COMMUNICATION STONES

GENERAL COMMUNICATION - Amazonite, Apatite, Chrysoprase, Copper, Clear Quartz Crystals, Emerald, Flint, Labradorite, Soulmate Crystals, Tabular Crystals, Turquoise.

CHANNELING ABILITIES - Calcite (gold), Channeling Crystals, Copper, Extra-Terrestrial Crystals, Kyanite, Meteorites, Pyrite, Sugilite, Tourmaline.

COMMUNICATION WITH SPIRIT GUARDIANS - Celestite, Channeling Crystals, Lapis Lazuli, Rutilated Quartz, Spirit Guardian Crystals, Star Sapphire, Tabular Crystals, Tourmaline, Window Crystals.

171

OPENNESS - Amazonite, Celestite, Lapis, Lifepath Crystals.

THE MYSTIC STONES

GENERAL PSYCHIC ABILITY - Amethyst, Azurite, Crystal Balls, Double Terminated Crystals, Herkimer Diamonds, Labradorite, Lapis Lazuli, Left-Handed Crystals, Merlin Crystals, Milky Quartz, Meteorites, Moonstone, Selene Crystals, Selenite.
CLAIRVOYANCE - Amazonite, Azurite, Emerald.
PAST LIFE RECALL - Amber, Amethyst, Carnelian, Garnet (red), Obsidian, Phantom Crystals, Sardonyx.
PROPHECY, DIVINATION - Amazonite, Aquamarine, Azurite, Crystal Balls, Double Terminated Crystals, Sapphire.
ASTRAL PROJECTION - Calcite (gold), Double Terminated Crystals.

THE HEALING STONES

GENERAL HEALING - Agate, Amber, Amethyst, Aventurine, Azurite, Calcite (green), Citrine, Clear Quartz Crystals, Garnet (green), Hawk's Eye, Inner Child Crystals, Hera Crystals, Jasper, Malachite, Peridot, Receiving Crystals, Rhodochrosite, Ruby, Rutilated Quartz, Sugilite, Tourmaline, Turquoise.
CLEANSING, PURIFICATION - Amber, Alexandrite, Aquamarine, Azurite, Bloodstone, Copper, Clear Quartz Crystals, Crystal Clusters, Emerald, Fluorite, Garnet (green), Lapis Lazuli, Malachite, Obsidian (black), Peridot, Receiving Crystals, Selenite.
ENERGY - Amber, Chalcedony, Chrysoprase, Citrine, Copper, Eight-Faceted Crystals, Garnet (red), Gold, Herkimer Diamonds, Merlin Crystals, Peridot, Right-Handed Crystals, Ruby, Sardonyx, Turquoise.
STRENGTH - Amber, Agate, Aquamarine, Chalcedony, Citrine, Labradorite, Lapis Lazuli, Onyx, Petrified Wood, Tiger's Eye, Tourmaline, Turquoise.
LONGEVITY, RENEWAL - Alexandrite, Chrysoberyl, Chrysoprase, Diamond, Hera Crystals, Jade, Peridot, Petrified Wood.
BALANCE - Agate, Amber, Amethyst, Aventurine, Bloodstone, Chrysoprase, Coral (white), Diamond, Double Terminated Crystals, Eight-Faceted Crystals, Fluorite, Hematite, Jade, Jet, Kunzite, Malachite, Smoky Quartz, Sodalite, Tabular Crystals, Tiger's Eye, Tourmaline, Turquoise.
RELAXATION - Amber, Agate, Amethyst, Aventurine, Jasper, Peridot, Petrified Wood, Seven-Faceted Crystals, Rhodonite.

Afterword

A woman leaves her dwelling, a crystal in her hand. She walks the land in a time of drought. In this water-starved place her every footfall creates a tiny dust storm. She comes to a mountain and climbs slowly to its topmost pinnacle. There she places the crystal on the parched ground in a sacred manner. Then she dances a circle sunwise around the crystal. She sings a rain chant. She makes a prayer for life-giving water. She sends her song through the Crystal Spirit to the Storm Beings, for the sake of the people, for the sake of the birds and animals, for the sake of her sacred Earth Mother. The Crystal Spirit hears her prayer and amplifies it to the heavens.

This happened thirty thousand years ago. This happened today.

Oakland, California
September 21, 1988

173

Acknowledgements

To Steve, for believing I was a writer before I did and for his unfailing love and support.

To Zu, for his confidence in the uniqueness and worth of my message; for stapling and trimming the Crystal Wisdom booklets with me late into the night; for filling the workday with laughter and merriment through long hours at small compensation.

To Patrick, for incredible patience, encouragement, kindness, humor and advice throughout this book's making.

To Judith, for her presence as the goddess of inspiration for this book.

To Ralph, for such sensitive and intelligent editing; for always working to help writers on the mainstream's margins to find their voices.

To Ian and Norine, for their superb work at the word processor, despite my rushed deadlines and battered manuscripts.

To all my students over the years, for their willingness to dare and discover and play in the sacred circle.

WORKSHOPS WITH DOLFYN

Dolfyn teaches workshops and classes on Crystals, Shamanism, and Nature Spirituality in the San Francisco Bay area as well as nationally. For information write: Earthspirit, Inc., 6114 LaSalle Ave., Suite 362, Oakland, Ca. 94611.

SPOKEN WORD CASSETTES BY DOLFYN

CRYSTAL WISDOM: A BEGINNER'S GUIDE

This cassette inspires the beginner with all he or she needs to know to get started with crystals. In clear, beautiful prose, Dolfyn teaches the basic aspects of crystal lore, such as tuning, programming, healing, protecting, meditating and channeling energy with crystals.

SHAMANISM: A GUIDE TO DEVELOPING SACRED POWER

This cassette covers aspects of shamanism common to native and tribal people the world over, yet applicable to our own lives. How to: create a Medicine Wheel, go on a Vision Quest, retrieve your Animal Spirit Guardians, find your Sacred Clan Name, develop Sacred Power in harmony with Earth Mother, and more.

Earthspirit, Inc., offers the above cassettes for $9.95 each. Send check or money order (no cash) to: Earthspirit, Inc., 6114 LaSalle Ave., Suite 362, Oakland, Ca. 94611.

ABOUT THE AUTHOR

Dolfyn cares deeply about nature. Her concern expresses itself in her writing and in her active involvement with environmental and earth stewardship issues. Her writings grow naturally from her practical experience in teaching and advocating for nature and the Nature Spirits.

HERE IS A PREVIEW OF EXCERPTS FROM DOLFYN'S NEW BOOK

(TO BE PUBLISHED IN THE AUTUMN OF 1990)

SHAMANIC WISDOM:
Nature Spirituality, Sacred Power and Earth Ecstasy

SHAMANIC WORLDVIEW

Primal peoples from all over the world, such as Native American Indians and tribal peoples of Africa and South America, hold a shamanic worldview. These people have developed paths of psychic powers and spiritual wisdom that are over thirty thousand years old. These belief systems are variously called Earth Religion, Nature Spirituality or Shamanism.

Although each tribe or primal group has different specific elements that are unique to their path, the principle of shamanism is the same. This book attempts to distill the essence of the shamanic worldview and teach you how to walk a shamanic path.

Earth Mother is calling Her human children back to the ancient ways of shamanism so that we might heal ourselves and our planet. She beckons us to Her so that we might once again walk in balance and in reverence upon our sacred Earth Mother.

One fundamental realization must be ours to walk the shamanic path: everything that is natural on the earth is alive and conscious. Bear and Crystal, Cat and Oak, Salmon and Butterfly all have a wisdom and a consciousness that we can communicate with. When we attempt to base our lives on this kind of understanding, when we acknowledge the plants and animals and minerals as our relatives, we re-establish our natural connection to all living beings. We begin to communicate directly with and learn from the Nature Spirits, a primary source of shamanic wisdom and power.

This book will show you some ways to adopt the shamanic worldview as your own, to communicate with the Nature Spirits in the languages of emotion, humor, love and creativity--the languages they understand.

The Nature Spirits offer to share with us the power that brings clear water from deep in the rock ribs of Earth Mother, the power that creates the fragile strength of the spider's web, the power that swings the stars through their courses and swells the ocean tides. When we connect ourselves with the Nature Spirits, we learn how to be energized by their energy, to be filled with their power, to become wise with their wisdom. That transforms us. It transforms our relations with others. It transforms our world.

PRAYING, ASKING, INVOKING

Like many tribal and native peoples, when you follow a shamanic path, you will come to regard the animals and plants as your grandparents and the rocks and stones as your great grandparents. These beings have evolved long before the human species and have witnessed human evolution. So they know how much we need to learn from them and be guided by them. The past several hundred years have shown how destructive humans become when they divorce themselves from nature and try to go it alone. Clearly, it is time to renew our ancient bond with the Nature Spirits and to walk in the protection of their understanding and assistance.

We can renew these connections by praying to the Nature Spirits, invoking their aid and asking for their instruction. Some traditional peoples call this type of praying "sending a voice." You can do that, too. You can send your voice to the wise and ancient trees, plants, rocks and animals.

Many of us have not prayed in so long that we have no idea how to begin, but that is no problem. Just go out into your yard or to a park, touch any natural being that calls to you and speak from your heart: "Tree Spirits, please give me the strength and the stability I need to meet the challenges I now face," or, "Flower Spirits, please help me attract love into my life, for I am lonely." And when you are finished praying, be sure to give thanks.

When you pray to one tree, for example, you also call upon the spirit of all trees. These are the Tree Spirits. Nature Spirits hold in their very being the collective consciousness and wisdom of their species. Therefore, Nature Spirits make excellent teachers, guides and helpers. A Tree Spirit, for instance, represents the experience and understanding of all trees who are living or have ever lived. If a nature being does not live in your locale, you can visualize it and then say a simple, heartfelt prayer like, "Lion Spirits, grant me courage and boldness."

There are times, too, when you will call upon particular spirits to fill you with their strengthening and empowering energies. This is often referred to as invoking. Invocation is a form of prayer you use to call the powers of various spirit and nature beings into yourself. As you go through your daily life, you can invoke power and healing from these sources by emulating them. For example, if you are invoking the Tree Spirits, then stand as a tree, wave your arms over your head like leaves; imagine your feet rooted to the earth, and call upon the Tree Spirits to live in you. Here is a tree invocation I use. You could try it or, better yet, create your own.

TREE SPIRIT INVOCATION

TREE SPIRITS, I AM CALLING ON YOU.
TREE SPIRITS, BE HERE NOW!
I NEED YOUR STRENGTH AND STABILITY.
TREE SPIRITS, LIVE IN ME!

THE WAY OF THE ANIMAL SPIRITS

Walking the shamanic path means increasing your familiarity with nature. To help you get started, here is a partial list of animals and some of their specific powers and attributes to call upon when praying to them or invoking them.

BADGER: Badger is totally fearless. Call upon Badger for courage, boldness and the ability to hold on to what is yours.

BEAVER: Beaver builds canals, lodges and dams. Invoke Beaver when building anything: dreams, a new life, a career.

COYOTE: While most wild predators are diminishing,

Coyote thrives and increases because he is so adaptable. Pray to Coyote to help us adjust and thrive in any situation.

EAGLE: Just as Eagle soars high, so does she inspire our spirits to soar. And just as Eagle sees far, so does she foster perspective. Pray to Eagle for cosmic awareness, clarity of vision and the will to realize your highest self.

ELEPHANT: Elephants enjoy excellent memories, learning abilities, longevity and loyalty to each other. Call upon Elephant for these attributes.

HORSE: Horse's sense of vision is very wide. She can see all around herself easily. We invoke Horse medicine when we want to get a broad picture and gain perspective.

LEOPARD: Leopard's medicine has to do with speed, timing and camouflage. Call upon her for these powers.

MOUSE: Living close to the earth, Mouse notices every little thing as she forages for food. Invoke Mouse to learn to appreciate the little joys in life.

OTTER: Quickly and efficiently meeting his food demands each day, Otter has much time for fun and play. We can pray to Otter when we want to get a job done quickly and well. We also invoke Otter to open our hearts to joy, laughter and a sense of play.

WOLF: Since Wolf mates for life, call upon Wolf for romantic love to help you find your lifemate. Invoke Wolf spirit within you to increase your loyalty.

MEDICINE WHEEL: THE SACRED CIRCLE

Ancient stone carvings and other archaelogical evidence suggest that the circle is one of humankind's oldest and most elemental symbols. Many native peoples build their dwellings in a circular manner and then arrange those dwellings in a circle. (Some North American Indians refer to the sacred circle as a medicine wheel.)

The circle is humankind's greatest symbol of perfection and wholeness. The circle's very shape speaks to us of the turning and returning cycles of life and death and rebirth, of the sun and moon and seasons, of time and timelessness. The circle also symbolizes Earth Mother in Her roundness, fullness and abundance.

No wonder that so many different tribal peoples have used and continue to use the circle in their rituals and ceremonies. For when we make a circle, a sacred circle, we are creating a very special and powerful space—a space where our energies become focused and strengthened, a place where we share in the mysteries of body and spirit, of time and eternity.

HOW TO CREATE A SACRED CIRCLE
OR MEDICINE WHEEL

A VERY SIMPLE MEDICINE WHEEL

To create your own very simple sacred circle, you might take some cornmeal and spread it in a circle on the ground or surround yourself with a circle of crystals, twigs or any other natural thing that is sacred to you. Cast this medicine wheel in a clockwise (sunwise) direction, for this is the direction for increasing energy. Cast the circle in a sacred manner; that is, let your actions rise intentionally from your deep feelings of respect and affection for Earth Mother.

It is good to start the circle in the East, for this is the place where the sun rises, but you can begin your circle anywhere. As you create the circle it is good to state out loud your intentions. Speak simply and from the heart. For example, "Earth Mother, I create a sacred circle today, in your honor. May the power I raise here be for the good of all life."

When you have completed your circle, enter it. You can now call for aid from any positive deity, any Nature Spirit or your own ancestors. The circle simply acts as an amplifier of everything you do inside of it. When you call to the spirit realm in a sacred circle, you will be attended to! Therefore, make sure all that you say and do is positive and life affirming. For exampe, you might call upon Wolf Spirit to enter the circle and fill you with loyalty and courage. Or you could pray to your deceased grandmother to help or guide you. Or you might ask the Great Spirit to save all endangered animals. You might pray, ask, invoke, visualize or even dance and sing—or just talk to the spirit realm. You might also sit quietly and see if there is a message for you from the spirit realm. When you are finished, give thanks to all the spirits you called upon.

In "Shamanic Wisdom" Dolfyn continues to teach you how to apply the ancient native and tribal peoples' wisdom to your own life in such chapters as:

ANIMAL SPIRIT GUARDIANS *** VISION QUEST
FINDING YOUR SACRED CLAN NAME
SACRED POWER *** RAINBOW MEDICINE
THE WAY OF THE TREE SPIRITS ** PROTECTION
RHYTHM AND DANCE ** WORDS OF POWER
THE SEVEN DIRECTIONS *** THE DREAMTIME
MOON MOTHER*SEEING IN A SACRED MANNER
BECOMING YOUR OWN SHAMAN* SUN FATHER
GIFTING, GIVING THANKS, GIVING BACK
MEDICINE POWER